MW01137013

Junior ★ Master Horseman™

AMERICAN QUARTER
HORSE ASSOCIATION

American Youth Horse Council

www.ayhc.com 800-879-2942 (800-TRY-AYHC)

Junior Master Horseman™
P.O. Box 200
Amarillo, TX 79168
jmh@aqha.org
806-376-4811

JuniorMasterHorseman.com

Table of Contents

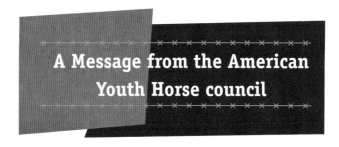

A Message from the American Youth Horse council

The American Youth Horse Council (AYHC) is proud to support the Junior Master Horseman™ (JMH) program with the American Quarter Horse Association (AQHA). AYHC is an umbrella organization providing encouragement, communication, leadership and resources to serve and promote the youth horse industry. This mission fits perfectly with what JMH is doing in regards to serving all levels of horse enthusiasts, especially those just starting on their horse adventure.

AQHA and AYHC believe that Kids + Horses = Magic. The Junior Master Horseman program exemplifies this statement by providing fun and educational materials and games in both a printed and electronic format for kids of all ages to be able to learn from and enjoy. The American Youth Horse Council hopes you enjoy your adventure with the Junior Master Horseman program and get started connecting with horses today! For more information on AYHC please visit www.ayhc.com or call 800-TRY-AYHC.

American Youth Horse Council
www.ayhc.com 800-879-2942 (800-TRY-AYHC)

Forward

The American Quarter Horse Association's *Junior Master Horseman™ program* was created, first and foremost, to bring the world of horses into the lives of children and horse enthusiasts interested in learning about horses. *Junior Master Horseman™: Level One* presents basic age-appropriate and kid-tested activities, created specifically to encourage young horsemen to embrace beginning horsemanship in a meaningful, safe, and fun way. Horse or no horse, all participants can experience the dynamics of learning about "everything" horses at their own pace, individually or with a group.

Junior Master Horseman™ also provides parents, caretakers, adult leaders, and educators with a curriculum-based teaching tool. Information supporting JMH's program goals originated from an extensive array of horse industry resources, including the American Youth Horse Council's acclaimed *Horse Industry Handbook: A Guide to Equine Care and Management*. Horsemen can also further their knowledge and extend opportunities to learn more about horses and horsemanship by visiting JMH's kid-friendly Web site at ***www.JuniorMasterHorseman.com***.

More than a valuable guide for introducing children to the equestrian way of life, Junior Master Horseman empowers children with useful ways and ideas to safely interact with their horse, or the horse they dream of someday owning!

Enjoy the experience of spending time with your young horseman as you work together through this book. It's the hope of every contributor to its content and design that it will provide opportunities for every participant to discover their own uniqueness, purpose, and future within the amazing world of horses.

~ Teri Vestal, JMH Author

Meet the JMH Crew!

Zak, Zap, and Zip
Troublemaking horseflies

Maisy
The wise spider

Concho
The all around horse

Hoss
The ranch boss cat

Tiny
The city slicker
English Bulldog

Skitter
The ornery barn rat

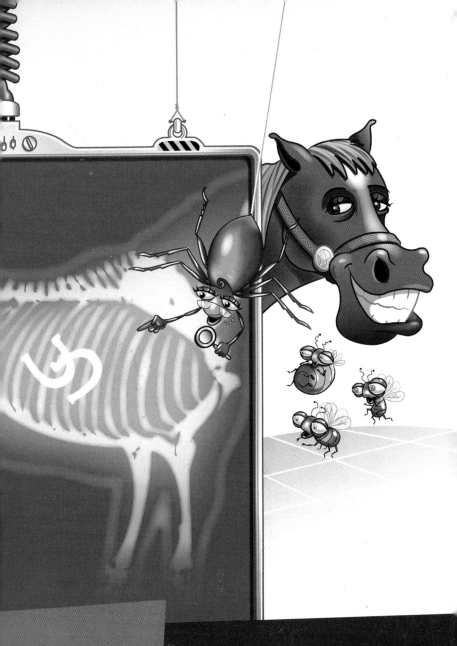

Chapter
1
★

Introduction
to Horses

Origin and Basics ✕ ✕ ✕ ✕ ✕ ✕ ✕ ✕

The Arrival and Departure of the First Horse

For millions of years, the horse has grazed Earth, evolving to become one of man's most useful and beloved companions. But have you ever wondered what the first horse looked like and where it lived?

Eohippus (Dawn Horse)

Meet Eohippus, also known as the Dawn Horse. This prehistoric ancestor of today's modern horse grazed the forested regions of North America over 50 million years ago. It stood only 10-20 inches tall, about the size of a fox, with three toes on its hind feet and four toes on its front. Fossils show that these Ice Age horses spread to every continent in the world, except Australia, and developed into many different species of horses around the world.

Eohippus continued to develop into a dog or deer-like animal with a more sloped neck, stronger teeth, longer legs, and it began to travel on its middle toe. As recently as 3 to 4 million years ago, horse-like Eohippus evolved into Equus, (around 13 hands tall) resembling today's large-headed, single-hoofed horse. Then for some unknown reason, around 10,000 years ago, horses disappeared altogether from the Americas, probably due to climate changes or excessive hunting by humans.

Fossils show us that horses lived millions of years ago right here in North America. In the following activity, a human fossil, or hoof print will be made and ideas will be shared about what kind of information fossils can show us about life lived so long ago. In the following activity, a human foot imprint will be made to represent a fossil.

Make Your Own Fossil Hoof Print

Objective: To create a dimensional human "hoof print"

Time: 45 minutes

Materials: Plaster of Paris; foot-size shallow container (tin pan); non-stick cooking spray

Saddle Up: Mix plaster according to directions. Cover inside of container with non-stick spray. Pour plaster into container. When plaster is almost "set," gently press bare foot ¾ of the way into mixture. Be careful to not press foot all the way through the plaster. Remove foot and clean. Before plaster dries, write name, age, and date into "fossil".

Variations:

★ Add color pigment while mixing plaster.

★ Paint and decorate dried plaster.

★ Use play dough or mud to make other kinds of "fossils."

Keep going!

Trail Talk: Have you ever tracked an animal, or found an animal print. What kind of information did that print reveal? Talk about how fossils are important and how they help us solve the mysteries of life from the past.

Ride Further: Explore horse Origins and Basics further by using these ideas:

★ Use a real horseshoe to make a lasting imprint in Plaster of Paris.

★ Create a simple poem about the history of the horse.

Horse Lingo

★ Simply put, the word **equid** is another term meaning horse.

★ The horse is classified as an **herbivore,** or plant eater.
   Note: Although "herbivore" begins with a consonant, the initial sound is that of a vowel and can be found proceeded with both "an" and "a" in various Texas adopted science texts. My personal preference is "an" due the auditory vowel sound.

★ The horse is a natural **herd animal**; one that likes to live in a group of its same kind.

★ **Mustang** comes from the Spanish word **mesteno**, which means ownerless.

The Horse Returns

So when did the horse return to North America? It wasn't until the early 1500s when seafaring Spanish conquistadors set out to explore and settle the New World. Amazingly, they loaded their horses and sailed for months on end, crossing the Atlantic Ocean. The Mustang, North America's feral (wild) horse, is a descendent of these horses brought to the New World. Later, European settlers crossed their horses with the Mustang to produce larger working horses, creating outstanding breeds like the American Quarter Horse, Appaloosa, Palomino, and the Pinto.

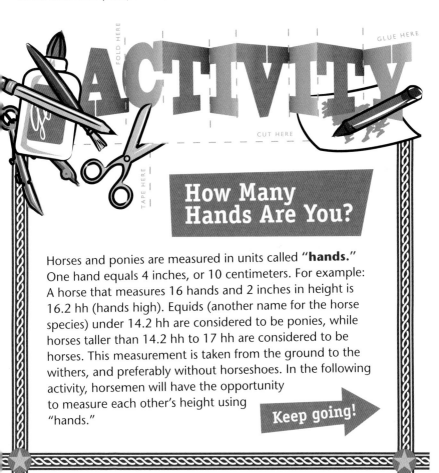

FOLD HERE   GLUE HERE

ACTIVITY

CUT HERE

TAPE HERE

How Many Hands Are You?

Horses and ponies are measured in units called **"hands."** One hand equals 4 inches, or 10 centimeters. For example: A horse that measures 16 hands and 2 inches in height is 16.2 hh (hands high). Equids (another name for the horse species) under 14.2 hh are considered to be ponies, while horses taller than 14.2 hh to 17 hh are considered to be horses. This measurement is taken from the ground to the withers, and preferably without horseshoes. In the following activity, horsemen will have the opportunity to measure each other's height using "hands."

Keep going!

Objective: To become aware of what a standard horse hand measurement is, and to practice measuring others using this unit of measurement

Time: 30 minutes

Materials: Poster board; scissors; group chart for recording measurements

Saddle Up: For a group activity, divide horsemen into pairs or small groups. Share that a standard horse hand (4 inches or 10 centimeters) is about the size of an average adult hand. Model how to measure hands by asking a volunteer to stand tall while the hand pattern is moved, one on top of another, from the foot (hoof) to the top of the shoulder (withers). Each horseman will cut out a hand pattern (see page 9) and take turns measuring each other.
Record and compare measurements.

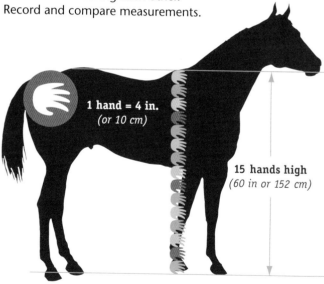

1 hand = 4 in.
(or 10 cm)

15 hands high
(60 in or 152 cm)

Keep going!

Trail Talk: Ask horsemen to share their knowledge about measuring hands. Then guesstimate how many hands other people, animals, or objects are.

Ride Further: Horses come in many different shapes, colors, and sizes and can be put into different groups. Three of these main types of horses are: Ponies; light horses; and draft horses. Read the following facts to discover which group your horse belongs to!

Ponies
Ponies stand under 14.2 hands high and weigh from 500 to 900 pounds. Ponies make great mounts for young children and are often used on trail rides, and in parades and exhibitions. Popular pony breeds include the American Shetland, Hackney, Highland, and Welsh.

Light Horses
Light horses stand from 14.2 to 17 hands high and weigh from 900 to 1400 pounds. They are used mostly for riding, racing, or driving and herding work. They are known for their exceptional performance abilities and include breeds like: The American Quarter Horse, Appaloosa, Arabian, Thoroughbred, and Tennessee Walking Horse.

Draft Horses
Draft horses stand 14.2 to almost 18 hands high and weigh 1,400 pounds or more. They are extremely muscular and strong, and used mostly for pulling heavy loads and working uneven, rocky, or boggy land. Some of these stout breeds include the Clydesdale, Lithuanian, and Shire.

Keep going!

If the shoe fits, wear it!

Circle the horseshoe and horse type that best fits your horse.

Pony

Light

Draft

I am sure that _____ is a _____ horse
          (your horse's name)   *(horse type)*

because (list facts from above) _____

_____

_____ .

Ride even further by using your knowledge about grouping horses to classify pet animals (birds, dogs, cats, etc.) into different groups based on size, weight, and individual traits.

TRIM HERE ✂

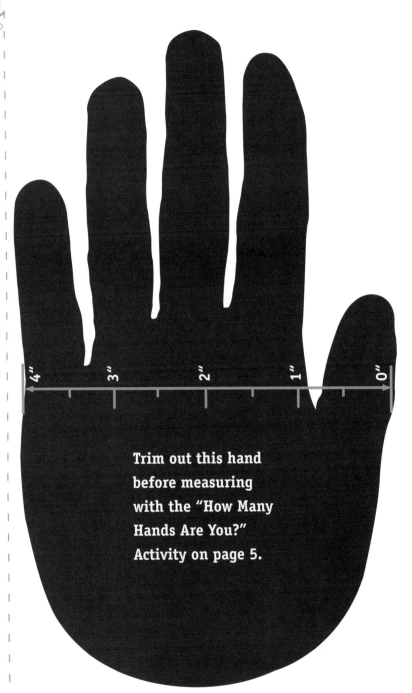

4" 3" 2" 1" 0"

Trim out this hand before measuring with the "How Many Hands Are You?" Activity on page 5.

Use the graphic on the other side of this page with the "How Many Hands Are You?" Activity on page 5.

Rein in Language (Journal Writing)

Imagine that you are a Spanish shipmate and it is your responsibility to tend to the Spanish conquistadors' horses while crossing the Atlantic Ocean to America. Write about your day.

Write a short description of your dream horse. Be sure to name your horse's breed classification, its markings, color(s), and what kind of temperament it has.

Just think...

If horses have been evolving since prehistoric times, who's to say they are not still changing right before your eyes? Draw a picture of what you think a horse might look like millions of years from now.

Barn Talk!

Imagine Native Americans without horses! Talk about how their way of life and culture would have been different if horses had not been brought to America by the Spanish.

Chapter 1: Introduction to Horses

FOLD HERE

GLUE HERE

CUT HERE

TAPE HERE

The Measure of a Miniature Horse

According to breed standards, the withers of an adult miniature horse are to not exceed 34 inches in height, which would make it about the size of a large dog. The miniature horse has a pleasing personality, and is often used in competition events like driving, jumping obstacles, and halter showing. In the following activity, a stick model of a miniature horse will be made out of paper.

Objective: To make a paper stick model of a miniature horse

Time: 45 minutes

Materials: Miniature horse picture; full newspaper stack (or brown packaging paper); masking tape; markers; yarn; scissors

Saddle Up: Did you know that Great Danes and Miniature Horses have something in common? Well, they do. As adults, they are just about the same height and not well suited for riding. Okay, enough about dogs. Stand a wooden yardstick

Keep going!

upright and make a mark at the 34-inch line. The adult Miniature Horses shouldn't exceed this mark (34 inches) in height in order to be registered. In the horse world, Miniature Horses are very unique and CAN be used and enjoyed much like full-grown horses. Use your noggin to think of ways that Miniature and full-size horses are alike and different. In the following activity, paper will be used to build a small-scale Miniature Horse.

For a group, each group will need 1 roll of masking tape and enough newspaper (5 2-page sections with a fold) to make five tubes. Follow these steps to build a paper stick horse frame:

★ With newspaper section flat (2 pages with fold), begin rolling one corner until a tube is made. Roll and tape 5 tubes.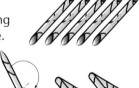

★ Fold 2 tubes in half to make "V" frames for the front and back legs.

★ Attach folded point of "V" frames to backbone tube. Tape and secure.

Keep going!

★ Fold another tube into a "V" for the neck. Attach and secure open end with tape to "withers," leaving the folded point at the top.

★ Fold another "V" and attach to neck for head. The open end will be the ears.

★ Cut, tie, and attach yarn mane and tail.

★ Don't forget to name your Miniature Horse(s). Option: Add color by painting body, markings, hooves, nose, eyes, etc.

Trail Talk: Name other animals that are about this same height as the Miniature Horse. What other animals have alike characteristics as the Miniature Horse (four legs, single hooves, herbivore, etc.).

Ride Further: Interesting facts about a horse's natural instincts:

★ Horses are naturally friendly animals.
★ Horses have a natural instinct to bond with other horses.
★ Wild horses feel safer living in a herd.
★ A dominant stallion will protect and breed with several mares in his herd.
★ Horses show affection to other horses by grooming each other.
★ Most of the time, horses stand close to one another while grazing.

Keep going!

★ Horses communicate with each other with body language like moving ears, swishing tails, and using their voices.

★ Horses sleep standing up. But for those horses lying down, there are usually other horses close by standing guard.

For more fun, go to *www.JuniorMasterHorseman.com*

PHOTOS COURTESY OF AMERICAN MINIATURE HORSE ASSN.

Did You Know?

★ When Christopher Columbus landed in the New World in 1492, he saw Native Americans, but no horses! It wasn't until the Spanish conquistadors began arriving in America in the early 1500s that horses were introduced to Native Americans.

★ For centuries, the miniature horse breed has been bred for pets, royal gifts, research, sale and profit, mining work, and exhibitions.

★ Zebras, donkeys, burros, and mules are just some of the other horse species that developed from the Dawn Horse.

The Importance of Horses

Just saying the horse has been important to man is not enough! For thousands of years, the horse has given man a dependable, fast way to move from one place to another. Hunters have chased their prey and soldiers have charged horseback into battle. American pioneers have hitched sturdy teams to pull wagons and stagecoaches from east to west, and the Pony Express delivered mail horseback long before today's type of mail delivery was even a thought. So, to say the horse has been just important is simply not enough!

Today, the horse isn't used as much for transportation, hunting, or rushing messages by Pony Express. However, it is important in equally exciting ways. People all over the world enjoy horses for recreation, work, sport, and entertainment. Perhaps you, or someone you know, ride in competitions, train, race, or saddle up for therapeutic or health reasons. Why, horses have even become famous movie stars like The Lone Ranger's horse, Silver, and Roy Roger's horse, Trigger.

PONY EXPRESS !

CHANGE OF   REDUCED

TIME!   RATES!

10 Days to San Francisco!

LETTERS

WILL BE RECEIVED AT THE

OFFICE, 84 BROADWAY,

NEW YORK,

Up to **4** P. M. every **TUESDAY,**

AND

Up to **2½** P. M. every **SATURDAY,**

Which will be forwarded to connect with the PONY EXPRESS leaving ST. JOSEPH, Missouri,

Every **WEDNESDAY** and **SATURDAY** at **11 P. M.**

TELEGRAMS

Sent to Fort Kearney on the mornings of MONDAY and FRIDAY, will connect with PONY leaving St. Joseph, WEDNESDAYS and SATURDAYS.

EXPRESS CHARGES.

LETTERS weighing half ounce or under..............$1 00
For every additional half ounce or fraction of an ounce 1 00
In all cases to be enclosed in 10 cent Government Stamped Envelopes,
And all Express CHARGES Pre-paid.
☞ PONY EXPRESS ENVELOPES For Sale at our Office,

WELLS, FARGO & CO., Ag'ts.

New York, July 1, 1861.

SLOTE & JANES, STATIONERS AND PRINTERS, 61 FULTON STREET, NEW YORK.

Ranked among the most remarkable feats to come out of the American West, the Pony Express was in service from April 1860 to November 1861. Its primary mission was to deliver mail and news between St. Joseph, Missouri, and Sacramento, California.

183 men are known to have ridden for the Pony Express during its operation of just over 18 months with the oldest, 40, and the youngest, only 11.

Have you ever mailed a letter and wondered how it gets to where it's going? In 1860, long before postal workers moved the mail like they do today, courageous young horsemen carried letters from one point to the next until their destination was reached. This service was known as the Pony Express. These young riders faced many dangers, such as thieves, extreme weather conditions, and over 1900 miles of rugged land. They rode day and night using the moon's light or flashes of lightening to keep the mail moving across the country…no matter what!

Fascinating facts about the Pony Express:

★ Riders followed a route from Sacramento, California, to St. Joseph, Missouri.

★ Riders were able to keep horses running at full speed for most of the distance by mounting a rested horse about every 10 miles along the route.

★ This service was the first main United States postal link between the east and west.

★ Relay stations were placed about every 10 miles, with the third station being where fresh horses, firearms, and provisions (food and supplies) were kept. It was also here that the mail would be handed over to a new rider.

★ The Pony Express had about 400 ponies and over 200 stations and was started up and ready for business in about two months.

Ride the Pony Express!

In this activity, horsemen will play a fun group game to better understand how Pony Express riders rode cross-country to deliver the mail.

Objective: To better understand Pony Express history and method of moving the mail

Time: 35 minutes

Materials: Several brooms, mops, or yardsticks; watch with second hand; old postcard, letter, small package; provisions (snacks, first aid, supplies, etc.); United States map with states, mountains, rivers, and land markings for tracing Pony Express route.

Saddle Up: Look at the Pony Express Map. Imagine riding along with one of the many brave Pony Express riders! Make your own Pony Express adventure come to life by finding an area outside to ride your own imaginary Pony Express route and following these steps:

1. Mark Pony Express exchange stations with bandanas or flags; three stations for mounting a fresh horse with a new rider being ready at every third horse.

Keep going!

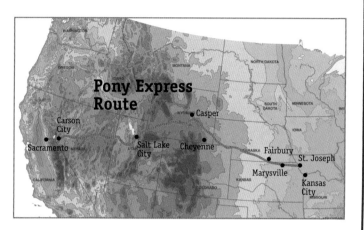

2. For a group, divide into small even groups. The goal will be for each Pony Express rider to safely and quickly carry mail along the route. Make sure everyone understands the route and routine of changing horses and riders.

3. Place game horses and provisions at stations.

4. Take your position at the starting line. The word to start the race will be "giddy up!" This is a fun timed race for an individual or group.

Now, get going and run the route as fast as you can! (Be sure to replace provisions for other riders)

Trail Talk: Talk about what kind of provisions might have been left at each third station of the real Pony Express. How would today's provisions be different from those used during the Pony Express days? Remember: Provisions could be human or equine food, drink, first aid supplies, tack, etc.

Keep going!

Ride Further: The U.S. Postal Service has an amazing history to explore in many fun ways!

★ Use a U.S. map to mark a route that might have been similar to the one traveled by Pony Express riders. Explain that the route could not be as the crow flies (straight line), but instead had to follow the lay of the land.

★ Create a newspaper article and illustration advertising the Pony Express.

★ Explore more about the exciting history of the U.S. Postal Service by visiting the Smithsonian Web site: ***www.postalmuseum.si.edu***

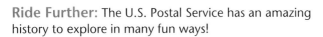

Make a movie!
Who's to say you and your horse might not be famous some day? If you and your horse could star in a movie, what would the movie be called and what would it be about? Maybe you should think about getting out the video camera and making your own horse movie!

Rein in Language (Journal Writing)

Think about how horses have changed the way people travel. Imagine you live back in the day when kids walked, traveled by wagon, or rode horses to school. Write about getting your horse ready, riding your horse to school, and how you care for your horse during the school day.

Horse Lingo

★ What's a *horseless carriage* or an *iron horse?*
Answer: A *train* or *car,* of course!

★ The Pony Express was known to many during its day simply as *The Pony.*

★ The Latin word *cursus* means running and the word *courser* is another word for spirited horse.

Did You Know?

★ Scottish inventor, James Watt (1736-1819), coined the term *horsepower*. The *watt*, a unit of electrical power, was also named for him.

★ A space shuttle's main engine power is equivalent to 12,000,000 horses!

★ The Pony Express lasted less than two years and was replaced by more modern methods of communication like the telegraph and railway service.

Howdy Horsemen!

Don't forget to wrangle your parents up to the computer and register at **www.JuniorMasterHorseman.com!**

Horse Anatomy ×—×—×—×—×—×—×—×—×—

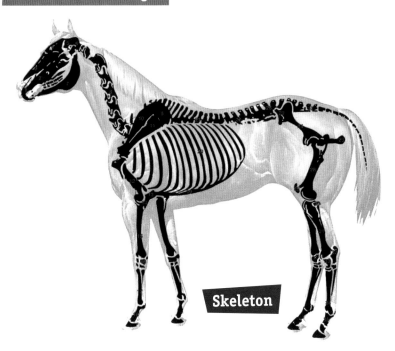

Skeleton

The Amazing Build and Keen Senses of the Horse

A horse's skeletal build is directly linked to its conformation (appearance) and performance. With a sturdy back and powerful hindquarters, long neck and sloping shoulder, and agile legs with long tendons and ligaments, the horse is able to carry its own weight and move in amazing ways.

Not only is a horse built to be a performer and useful companion, but this intelligent animal is also equipped with keen senses of smell, touch, and sight. Whether friend or foe, the horse will quickly pick up your scent, just as

he/she will also sense the smell of food or water from a good distance away.

Sneaking up on a horse isn't an easy thing to do, and certainly not recommended! But have you ever noticed how quickly a horse can sense that someone or something is nearby without even turning a head? Proceed with caution if you hear your horse softly whinny, or you see those eye balls turn, ears perk, and the tail restlessly swishing. In its own language, the horse is simply saying…I know you're there, so watchout!

Awesome Anatomy

You may have more in common with your horse than you think! For example, humans and horses share some common body part names such as nostrils, foreheads, lips, knees, and elbows. In the following activity, horse body parts will be named and labeled on a horse picture.

Objective: To identify parts of the horse's anatomy and play a timed game of attaching labels on a horse picture

Time: 30 minutes

Materials: Horse picture complete with labeled body parts (see page 28); Horse picture (see page 29); body part labels (see page 31); tape. Suggestion: Laminate pictures and labels

Saddle Up: Using the labeled horse picture, find and name each body part. Then take turns timing each other in a race to correctly place each body part label on the horse picture.

Trail Talk: Make a list of things that horse owners can do to keep their horse(s) healthy and sound.

Ride Further:
★ A horse's forelimbs (front legs and upper front body) bear 65% of a horse's weight. Ask horsemen to use their

Keep going!

math skills to find out how much remaining percentage of weight is left to be carried by other parts of the horse's anatomy.

★ Have fun comparing human and horse anatomy by finding similarities and differences on a skeletal horse and human picture model.

★ Learn the importance of equine dental care as well as the proper, safe way to check your horse's teeth (and age) by taking a trip to the local veterinarian. This can also be done by inviting an adult experienced with working with horses to demonstrate his/her knowledge and methods of caring for horse teeth.

Horse Lingo

★ *Peripheral* vision is the medical term that also means *field of vision.*

★ The term *conformation* refers to a horse's skeletal structure and overall appearance.

★ A horse with *well-sprung* ribs has a nicely rounded ribcage to hold and protect the heart and lungs.

Dentists for Horses...

Barn Talk!

Like humans, horses need a dental check-up at least twice each year. Routine visits to the veterinarian or equine dentist for floating, or the filing of sharp points that might cause discomfort to the horse, can help keep a horse's mouth in the best condition possible...and that's something worth chewing on!

Rein in Language (Journal Writing)

Write about the last time you took your horse to the veterinarian. Tell why your horse needed medical attention and when you expect to return with your animal to see the veterinarian again. For extra fun, draw a map showing the path you take from your house to the veterinarian's clinic.

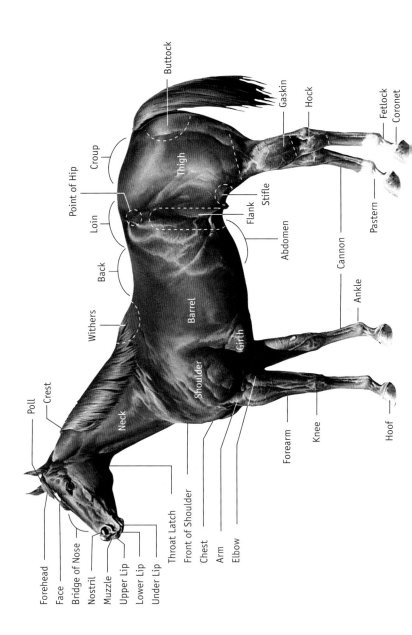

Buttock

Gaskin

Hock

Fetlock

Coronet

Croup

Thigh

Point of Hip

Stifle

Loin

Flank

Abdomen

Back

Pastern

Withers

Barrel

Cannon

Girth

Ankle

Crest

Poll

Shoulder

Neck

Knee

Hoof

Forearm

Forehead

Face

Bridge of Nose

Nostril

Muzzle

Upper Lip

Lower Lip

Under Lip

Throat Latch

Front of Shoulder

Chest

Arm

Elbow

Cut out the horse on the previous page and the following labels to use with the Awesome Anatomy Activity from page 25.

TRIM HERE ✂

Forehead	Chest	Loin	Hock
Face	Arm	Croup	Fetlock
Bridge of Nose	Elbow	Point of Hip	Coronet
Nostril	Forearm	Neck	Abdomen
Muzzle	Knee	Shoulder	Cannon
Upper Lip	Hoof	Barrel	Ankle
Lower Lip	Poll	Thigh	Pastern
Under Lip	Crest	Girth	Flank
Throat Latch	Withers	Buttock	Stifle
Front of Shoulder	Back	Gaskin	

Cut out the labels on
the back of this page to use
with the Awesome Anatomy
Activity from page 25.

Did You Know?

★ Horses are able to sleep standing up due to the ligaments and tendons that run down their legs, giving them the ability to "lock" their joints in place.

★ A horse's skeleton is made up of approximately 205 bones, close to the same amount as the human skeleton of 206 bones.

★ When horses roll their lips back, it is their way of distinguishing different smells more clearly...and you thought they were just laughing!

★ A red ribbon tied on the tail is a sure sign of an experienced kicker, so watch out!

Hey Horse Buddies!

Come along with me to **www.JuniorMasterHorseman.com!** Don't forget to ask permission!

Donkey Out —Horse In!

Most everyone has played the traditional birthday game known as Pin the Tail on the Donkey. To continue learning more about the horse's amazing anatomy, horse around with a newer, more equine-tastic version of this entertaining game. In the following activity, the horse's tail and other parts of the horse's anatomy will be placed on a horse picture by a blindfolded horseman.

Objective: To use knowledge of the horse's anatomy to place cut-out body parts on an identical horse picture

Time: 30-45 minutes

Materials: Tape; blindfold; two enlarged copies of the JMH Anatomical Horse picture, one labeled with body parts (see page 37) and one without (see page 39). One picture will be used for hanging and one will be cut up for horsemen to place individual parts onto the hanging horse picture in a new game version of Pin the Tail on the Donkey.

Saddle Up: This is a really fun group game, but can also be enjoyed with two horse buddies. First, cut up one of the JMH Anatomical Horse pictures and place tape on the back of each piece. Pin up the other JMH Anatomical Horse picture.

Keep going!

Talk about the name and purpose (or function) of each labeled body part, how they make a horse unique, and help the horse perform. Before playing the game blindfolded, encourage horsemen to practice placing body part names on the horse using their sight. Body parts will be placed on the horse picture using only verbal clues. Blindfold horseman and turn several times in place. Head the blindfolded horseman in the direction of the horse picture. Give verbal clues to help the horseman place the body part name as close to the matching point on the horse picture as possible. Variation: This can also be played without the blindfold and made into a fun timed individual or group game.

Trail Talk: As each body part is removed from the hanging picture, encourage horsemen to share the name and purpose (or function) of each body part.

Ride Further:
★ Use a zebra, also in the horse family, pattern for a fun game of Pin the Stripes on the Zebra

★ To check comprehension and understanding, provide horsemen with a list of body parts. Then invite horsemen to fill-in the unlabeled JMH Anatomical Horse picture.

★ Using a JMH Anatomical Horse picture, cut out horse body parts. Paint pieces with glow-in-the-dark paint. Puzzle and glue horse picture back together on black construction paper to create a glowing work of horse art.

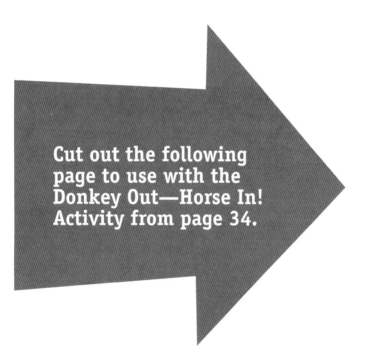

Cut out the following page to use with the Donkey Out—Horse In! Activity from page 34.

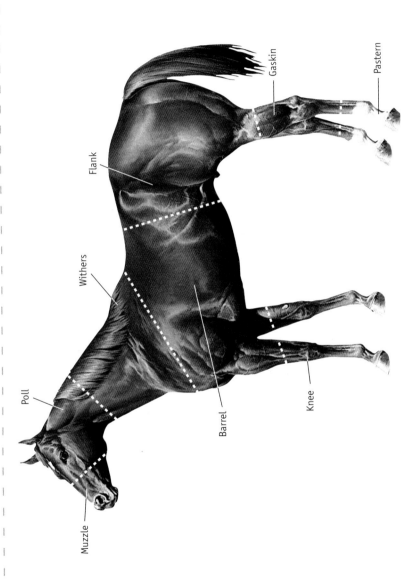

37

Cut out the following page to use with the Donkey Out—Horse In! Activity from page 34.

TRIM HERE

Cut out the image on the back of this page and use with the Donkey Out—Horse In Activity from page 34.

Chapter
2★

Breeds, Color
Patterns & Types

Breeds ✕ ✕ ✕ ✕ ✕ ✕ ✕ ✕ ✕ ✕ ✕ ✕

What Exactly is a Breed?

A breed is an animal group with many of the same characteristics. Horses in a breed may have the same appearance (conformation), hand height, and stride. They may also have similar color patterns and markings. All of these unique features play an important role in identification and breed registration.

Horse breeds, old and new, can be as different as horses themselves, which makes learning about them all the more interesting! Take a look at these two amazing and very different horse breeds, the Arabian and Azteca:

PHOTO COURTESY OF ARABIAN HORSE ASSN.

Photo: Anne Young

Arabian

The Arabian breed originated in Africa and the Far East and is probably one of the most pure,

or natural, breeds. This ancient breed dates back to Biblical times and is included in Egyptian art from thousands of years ago. Arabians have long been known for their ability to endure harsh desert climates and easily travel across desert lands.

Azteca

In contrast, the Azteca breed is one of the more modern, or artificial, breeds. The Azteca was the first breed developed in Mexico and was officially registered by Mexico's Department of Agriculture in 1982. The Azteca is a cross between Andalusian, American Quarter Horse, and Criollo, and is known for having an excellent temperament and being a fine dressage competitor.

Here's a good question to ponder

How many horse breeds are there around the world? Think about ways that a worldwide count of horse breeds, registered and non-registered, could accurately be taken. Then if you can't stand waiting for someone else to discover this somewhat unknown number ... go ahead, use your own ideas and find out for yourself!

Barn Talk!

Take a look at the following chart to see how the major breeds compare with each other. Keep in mind that there are many breeds of horses, and not all are represented on this chart.

2003 Major Breed Registrations

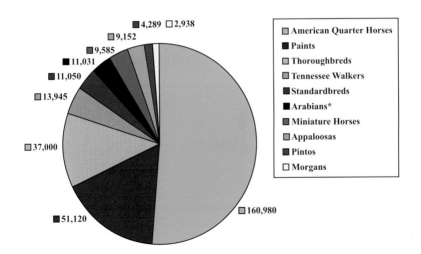

*Includes Half-Arabians and Anglo - Arabians as well as purebreds.

Howdy Pardners!

You and your parents can learn more about horse breeds by visiting the American Youth Horse Council's Web site at ***www.ayhc.com***

ACTIVITY

FOLD HERE GLUE HERE CUT HERE TAPE HERE

Horse Breeds Word Find

Objective: To identify horse breed names in written text

Time: 20 minutes

Materials: Horse Breeds Word Find (on page 45) and answer key (see appendix)

Saddle Up: Have fun researching and discovering different horse breeds using as many resources as you can. Review the breed names, then complete the word find. Use answer key to check.

Keep going!

Horse Breeds Word Find

```
N  F  X  W  J  K  R  T  H  B  N  C  V  Z  H
K  A  F  B  R  T  E  R  D  U  S  Q  L  D  U
C  X  I  C  C  L  Y  D  E  S  D  A  L  E  A
O  R  V  S  A  M  V  R  R  F  N  N  P  E
N  O  I  U  E  O  S  D  B  F  A  A  P  H  B
I  E  H  O  R  I  N  G  H  T  I  A  S  A  L
M  Z  R  G  L  A  R  Q  G  S  L  Q  A  C  I
O  L  A  I  L  L  K  F  U  O  T  O  K  K  P
L  N  B  T  H  R  O  L  O  T  N  I  P  N  I
A  L  E  E  T  S  A  S  R  B  K  D  H  E  Z
P  H  N  P  H  D  A  F  O  H  X  A  S  Y  A
S  I  I  Z  N  K  O  S  H  T  N  I  L  O  N
W  C  T  A  U  W  N  N  T  U  K  P  E  O  N
V  V  A  P  G  C  A  S  P  I  A  N  W  C  E
A  L  L  E  B  A  L  A  F  Q  J  F  W  P  R
```

Find These Breeds:

ANDALUSIAN	APPALOOSA	CASPIAN	CLYDESDALE
CRIOLLO	FALABELLA	FRIESIAN	HACKNEY
LIPIZANNER	MORGAN	PALOMINO	PINTO
SHETLAND	SHIRE	THOROUGHBRED	WELSH

(See appendix for answer key)

Trail Talk: Use memory to name as many horse breeds as you can. Then have fun using the letters of the alphabet to name horse breeds that begin with each letter.

Ride Further: Write horse breed names on small pieces of paper. Fold and place in a hat or boot. Take turns pulling out breed names and explore individual breeds by using the following resources:

★ *Horse Industry Handbook: A Guide to Equine Care and Management* (American Youth Horse Council)

Horse Lingo

★ *Hotbloods* are speedy, fine-boned horses with feisty temperaments descended from horses originally found in desert climates such as the Thoroughbred, Arabian, and Akhal-Teke.

★ *Warmbloods* are descended from larger, heavier horses and often named for the region in which they were bred such as the Hanoverian and Holsteiner from Germany.

★ *Coldbloods*, originating in North Europe, are a combination of hot and cold bloodlines and are known for being very strong and having docile temperaments.

★ *A grade horse* is one that is not registered or has an unknown ancestry.

Rein in Language (Journal Writing)

Santa needs to replace his team of eight tiny reindeer. Write about which horse breed(s) would most likely be the best choice(s) for Santa's Christmas Eve ride.

Did You Know?

★ The Shetland pony, Great Britain's oldest pony breed, is named after the islands where they originated, the Shetland Islands, located off the northern coast of Scotland.

★ The oldest European horse breed is the Lipizzaner (Austria).

★ The Falabella is the smallest horse in the world, standing under 9 hands high.

★ The breed name, Palomino, is also an official horse color name. Find out more about this interesting tidbit of information in the next section!

Color Patterns ✕ ✕ ✕ ✕ ✕ ✕ ✕ ✕ ✕ ✕

Each and every person has a unique combination of eye, hair, and skin coloring, and some people are blessed with freckles, birthmarks, and other individual characteristics that make them one-of-a-kind, matchless, irreplaceable! Same goes for the horse world. All horses, and many breeds, have unique markings and characteristics that also make them an individual work of art and a masterpiece of Mother Nature's amazing animal kingdom.

Just like people, horses have markings and characteristics that make them unique!

PHOTO COURTESY OF AQHA

PHOTO BY KEVIN ANDOW
PHOTO COURTESY OF
APPALOOSA HORSE CLUB (ApHC)

PHOTOS COURTESY
OF AQHA

Create a new horse breed!

Barn Talk!

If you could create a new horse breed with unique markings never seen before, what would this new breed look like and what would its name be?

ACTIVITY

FOLD HERE · GLUE HERE · CUT HERE · TAPE HERE

Face Markings: The Basics

Many horses are born with white patterned markings. These unique patterns of stark white color add to the horse's beauty and individual look, and are used as a way to identify a horse for breed registration. These markings can be anywhere on the horse's body and in any shape imaginable. However, markings on a horse's face usually fall into five basic shapes or a combination of these shapes:

★ **Star:** small diamond-shaped white marking on forehead

Keep going!

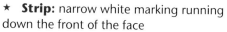

★ **Strip:** narrow white marking running down the front of the face

★ **Snip:** small white marking near the nostrils

★ **Blaze:** wide white marking extending from the forehead to the nostrils

★ **Bald face:** wide white marking covering a large area of the face

In the following activity, masks will be created to represent each basic marking, along with one combination marking.

Objective: To identify and create equine face markings through language and art

Time: 45 minutes

Materials: 6 paper plates per horseman; colored markers; 6 stick handles (tongue depressors or Popsicle sticks); glue; stapler

Saddle Up: Identify the five basic face markings. Then think about how any two of these markings could be put together to make a combination marking. To make the first mask, roll paper plate into a tubular shape. Staple or tape ends to create a tubular horse face. Repeat by rolling each plate until all six horse faces are made. Draw each of the five basic markings and one combination marking. Glue a stick handle on the back of each mask.

Keep going!

After the masks are completed, gather in a circle. Have someone call out each basic face marking. Horsemen will respond by holding up the correct horse mask. When combination markings are held up, describe markings used to create these unique patterns.

Trail Talk: Use masks to identify what kind of facial marking(s) are on horses at home. Remind horsemen that horses can also be solid in color and have no markings.

Ride Further:

★ Take a look at an official breed registration form and discover how markings are recorded in the registration process.

★ Study registration papers to memorize registered names and bloodlines.

★ Link up with favorite breed association site(s) and discover what kind of breed information and equine fun is there for everyone in the family to enjoy!

Horse Lingo

★ A *whorl* is a spiral pattern of horse hairs.

★ What's a *wall eye*? It's an eye that has a glassy blue or white coloring.

★ The *blue zone* is an area around a natural Paint marking that is bluish in color.

The Mark of Champions

Horses can also have distinctive leg markings. For example, The American Quarter Horse has four types:

★ **Coronet:** small white marking that circles, or bands, the leg right above the hoof

★ **Sock:** white marking that runs from the hoof halfway to the knee or hock

★ **Pastern/Half Pastern:** small white marking around the pastern (ankle)

★ **Stocking:** white marking that runs from the hoof up to the knee or hock

These patterns, or markings, can be on one, two, three, or all four legs. A horse also can have different markings on each leg. When a horse is registered the owner also must submit a picture of the horse so equine experts can carefully look at all of the horse's markings and record this important information. In this activity, leg markings will be named. Then a fun game using human socks to match horse markings will be played.

Objective: To identify basic leg markings, use auditory listening skills, and work cooperatively to play a game

Time: 30 minutes

Materials: 4 types of white socks: below ankle (coronet); ankle (pastern); crew (sock); and knee high (stocking). Each team will have one sock from each pair of the four types; one pair of socks will provide leggings for two teams.

Saddle Up: Pair up or divide into small groups. One horseman will get on all fours and pretend to be a horse. Each team will have an equivalent of one sock from each of the 4 types. Review which socks represent each basic leg marking:

★ Coronet - below ankle sock

★ Pastern - ankle sock

★ Sock - crew sock

★ Stocking - knee high sock

Toss all the socks into one big pile for everyone to pull from and encourage horsemen to listen carefully to the commands. The goal is for each group to choose the correct sock and quickly put it on the correct front or back leg of their horse partner without getting bum-fuzzled!

Keep going!

Command #1:

Left front leg - no mark   **Left back leg** - sock
Right front leg - no mark   **Right back leg** - stocking

Command #2:

Left front leg - no mark   **Left back leg** - coronet
Right front leg - sock   **Right back leg** - stocking

Command #3

Left front leg - coronet   **Left back leg** -stocking
Right front leg - sock   **Right back leg** - pastern

Trail Talk: Talk about how fun, easy, or challenging it was to follow each command. Talk about how important it is to be a good listener, especially when someone is sharing important information that could help improve your riding, grooming, or showmanship skills.

Ride Further:

★ Create more fun commands, change partners, and play the sock game again!

★ Label the JMH Leg Markings page (leg graphics with blank lines underneath for labeling)

★ Visit the veterinarian's office to observe different forms of identification such as computer chips, also implanted into dogs and cats, as well as lip tattooing and various other types of branding methods that help mark and identify horses.

Rein in Language (Journal Writing)

Describe your dream horse. First, name your dream horse and tell how you acquired him or her. Then use descriptive words (adjectives) to create a visual picture about your horse's size, color, markings, personality, and talents. Don't forget to capitalize your title, indent paragraphs, check punctuation, and use the dictionary to check for spelling errors.

FOLD HERE

GLUE HERE

CUT HERE

TAPE HERE

Painted Patterns

History tells us that Spanish explorer Hernando Cortez is responsible for the breed of horses known as the Paint. Actually, this breed came about as a result of one of his spotted sorrel and white war horses breeding with a Native American Mustang back in the early 1500s.

Keep going!

Also called pinto, skewbald, and piebald, this breed can be colored with distinctive patterns of stark white with black, brown, buckskin, bay, chestnut, dun, sorrel, palomino, roan, gray, grullo, cremello, and perlino.

Objective: To recognize three basic registered American Paint Horse patterns

Time: 20 minutes

Materials: Basic pattern information on tobiano, overo, and tovero; black and white patterned pictures

Saddle Up: Look at these registered coat patterns of the American Paint Horse. Read about the patterns called tobiano, overo, and tovero. Then use your knowledge to identify each pattern name with a black and white picture.

Tobiano
(pronounced: tow be yah' no)

This pattern may be either predominately dark or white. One or both flanks are usually covered with a dark color. All four legs are usually white, at least below the hocks and knees. Ovals or round patterns extend over and down the neck and chest, giving the appearance of a shield. Head markings may be solid, a blaze, strip, star, or snip. The tail is often two colors.

For a reminder of horse anatomy, see page 28.

Keep going!

Tovero
(pronounced: tow vair' oh)

This pattern has dark color around the ears, which may expand to cover the forehead and/or eyes. One or both eyes may be blue. Dark color is around the mouth, which may extend up the sides of the face and form spots. Spots on the chest can be varying sizes and may extend up the neck. Flank spots often also have smaller spots that extend forward across the barrel, and up over the loin. The base of the tail may also have spots.

Overo
(pronounced: oh vair' oh)

The white in this pattern usually will not cross the back of the horse between the withers and tail. At least one leg is dark, but often, all four legs are dark. Usually, the white is not even but scattered or splashy. Head markings are unique, often bald-faced, apron-faced, or bonnet-faced. An overo may be either mostly all dark or white. The tail is usually one color.

Keep going!

Now, which is which? Use your new knowledge of these three registered American Paint Horse patterns to choose the matching pattern name: tobiano, overo, or tovero.

_____   _____   _____

Trail Talk: Talk about how the colorful coat patterns of the Appaloosa, American Paint Horse and Pinto breeds are alike and different:

★ Appaloosa - Body can be any base color with spotted coat patterns over entire body and/or white blanket over hips with or without spots; muzzle and genitalia can be mottled; eye(s) can have sclera (ring around eye); and hooves can be striped.

★ Paint/Pinto - Body can be any base color and is a combination of white and colored markings; most common patterns are tobiano and overo.

Ride Further: There's so much more to learn about colorful horse breeds!

★ Visit a local museum or library to explore the use of the American Paint Horse in Native American art.

★ Find more interesting information about other American Paint Horse markings and patterns, history, and registration standards by logging onto the American Paint Horse Association Web site at ***www.apha.com***.

Did You Know?

★ Registration of a horse with the various breed associations is insurance to protect an owner's investment. Just like registering a car before you drive it, registering your horse confirms you are the owner. Additionally, it also certifies the horse's parentage, which greatly increases a horse's value. Registering a horse takes little time or money but can be a big benefit

★ Most horse hooves fall into three marking categories: white, black (or dark), and striped.

★ A dorsal stripe is a dark marking that runs down the horse's back and is common on dun and bay horses.

★ The Appaloosa, Paint, and Pinto breeds are considered not only color patterns but also color breeds.

Types

In the horse world, the term *type* refers to a horse or pony that is well-suited or bred for performing a particular job, and can belong, or not belong, to any specific horse breed. When man discovered that cross-breeding, or mixing breeds, could produce a specific kind of horse to fulfill a need or purpose, the horse's role changed … and so did history!

Drop the reins for a spell and just think about these historical images: Roman leaders racing in chariots pulled by sure-footed ponies; early travelers trekking in carriages and stagecoaches pulled by harnessed light horses or light (saddle) horses charging into battle carrying soldiers and mighty warriors; and farmers plowing fields and hauling heavy loads with powerful draft horses.

Yes! Times have changed and yesterday's horse has been replaced by today's high-tech engines and machinery. But horses today are still bred for size and strength, speed and disposition, as well as for many useful and rewarding purposes.

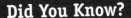

Did You Know?

★ The stock horse is one of the quickest, most agile and useful types of horse. Stock horses, like the American Quarter Horse, Appaloosa, and Paint, are athletic, great at handling cattle, and excellent in high-performance events.

★ The hack is considered one of the most majestic, elegant horse types, having superior conformation and presence.

★ The hunter, another notable horse type, is known for being courageous and intelligent. They have enduring stamina to carry riders for long periods of time.

Imagine Life in the Wild West!

Barn Talk!

Think back, long before the first train track was ever laid, about how the Wild West might have been different without horses. Imagine settlers crossing the country from east to west without wagons pulled by horses. Ponder what kind of animals ranchers would have used to herd cattle and what kind of transportation the Pony Express might have depended on, other than the horse, to deliver the mail. Discuss how the horse changed not only the Wild West's history, but America's history, too!

Rein in Language (Journal Writing)

You're just a content old pasture horse, not belonging to one breed or another, but it's always been your dream to belong to a registered breed. Write about which breed you would like to belong to and why.

Horse Lingo

★ The term *dark horse* is used to name an unexpected winner, or someone that most would consider not likely to win a competition.

★ If you see the term *ready to start* in an advertisement, beware! This most likely means that the horse for sale has never been ridden.

Maintenance

Shelter ⟶ ✕ ✕ ✕ ✕ ✕ ✕ ✕ ✕ ✕ ✕ ✕ ✕

Home Sweet Home

Horses are born with the natural instinct to follow a trail of feed and water, protect themselves, and seek shelter when they are threatened by severe weather. But for stalled horses, their ability to take care of their own needs is limited. Their welfare and safety are left in the hands of responsible owners and caretakers.

PHOTO COURTESY OF MD BARNS

Always keep your horse's safety in mind when considering where to pasture, board, and stall. Knowing how to provide your horse a safe shelter is an important part of horse ownership. Pastures should have reliable water sources, good grazing, and horse-friendly gates and fencing. Barns and stalls should be carefully planned and maintained so that a horse can live safely and comfortably for long periods of time.

✕ ✕ ✕ ✕ ✕ ✕ ✕ ✕ ✕ ✕ ✕ ✕ ✕ ✕

Overnight Shelters

Barn Talk!

Find out if there are any overnight shelters in your area for horsemen and their horses making long hauls. If not, then consider organizing a local shelter and registering it with a national directory.

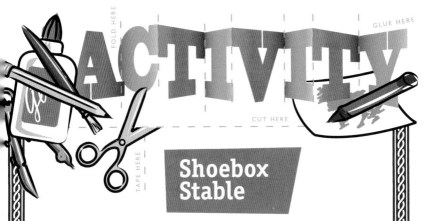

Shoebox Stable

Making sure a horse has shelter and protection from severe weather is important to any horse's well-being. Shelter to a horse is like a home to a horseman. Today's shelters can range from luxurious to simple: from an air-conditioned, well-bedded stall to the old porch of an abandoned ranch house. In the following activity, a simple model of a safe and protective horse shelter will be made using a shoebox.

Objective: To make a model of a horse shelter and recognize the importance of a safe and protective horse shelter

Time: 45 minutes

Materials: Small box or shoebox; toy horse or paper cut-out (pattern on page 67)

Saddle Up: Using a shoebox and a toy or paper horse, make a model of a horse shelter by using these suggestions:

★ If the shelter is enclosed, it should have enough room for the horse to turn around comfortably and be high enough that the horse doesn't bump its head.

★ Doors or gates should be wide enough for the horse to move in and out with ease.

Keep going!

★ Window(s) should open, close, and be placed high enough so the horse cannot jump through but be low enough so that the horse can see outside.

★ There should be good air circulation.

★ The roof should be built so rainwater drains away from the building.

Ideas for shoebox stable: Think about adding padding (quilted material) and bedding (confetti or pencil shavings).

Trail Talk: Name other ideas that could help make a horse's home more comfortable and safe.

Ride Further:

★ Measure and record measurements (dimensions) of other local horse facilities. Find square footage, which should not be less than 100 square feet, by multiplying the area's length x width.

★ Create an art gallery of interesting barns and favorite horses. Be sure to label, sign, and date each piece.

Barn Types

Turn-Out

PHOTO COURTESY
OF MD BARNS

Fancy Stable

Horse Pattern

Cut out these horses to help you design your shelter.

Use the graphic on the other side of this page with the "Shoebox Stable" Activity on page 65.

Could You Keep a Horse in Your Room?

If you could sneak your horse into your room to spend the night, would there be enough space? Horses need a minimum living space of approximately 10 feet wide by 10 feet long to be comfortable. In this activity, room measurements will be recorded and graphed to discover which rooms have enough space to comfortably stall a full-size horse.

Objective: To develop an awareness of the space (square footage) needed to properly stall a horse by using math measurement

Time: Unlimited

Materials: Tape measure; lined graph paper; ruler; pencil (use 10 x 10 grid on page 72 to help you)

Saddle Up: How much space (square footage) is needed to comfortably stall a horse? Take a guess at how much square footage (length x width) is in your bedroom.

Guess _____

Keep going!

Take a look at your graph paper's dimensional equivalents. Each square will represent a measurement, usually one foot. Use a ruler to draw a 10 X 10 square foot room. This is the size of stall that most horses need to be comfortable. Think about your horse's stall size. Knowing what you do now about how much room a horse needs to live comfortably, is your horse's home too small or just right?

Now, measure and record the square footage of these areas:

Bedroom _____ (length) X _____ (width) = _____ square feet

Horse stall ____ (length) X ____ (width) = _____ square feet

Could you comfortably keep a horse in your room?

Yes   No   *(circle one)*

Is your horse's stall roomy enough for more than one horse?

Yes   No   *(circle one)*

Trail Talk: Share ideas about other features that play a role in providing a good stall such as bedding, ventilation, and feed and tack storage.

Ride Further:

★ Visit a local horse farm or equestrian center to see how horses are stalled, fed, groomed, and exercised.

★ Design a new barn for your horse using your new graphing skills. (you can see a sample on the next page and create your own!)

★ Serve others by organizing a Horse Hand Work Day to help elderly or handicapped horsemen repair and muck out stalls.

Keep going!

Sample Barn Layout

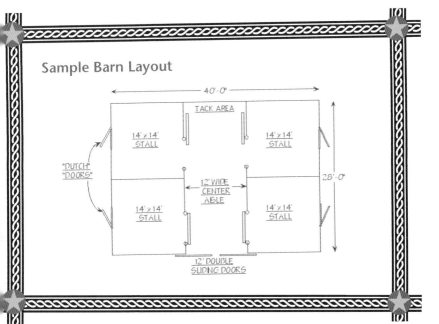

Horse Lingo

★ *Mucking out* is the process of thoroughly cleaning a horse's stall.

★ Ever heard anyone say, *"Hold your horses?"* If so, you might listen because, for some reason, they are cautioning you to wait and not make a move!

★ What's a *run-in*? It's simply a roofed three-sided shed often used in a pasture to give livestock shelter.

★ Does your horse have a *vice*? A vice is a bad habit or undesirable behavior, like chewing on the fence, kicking, or running away at the sight of the halter. Most vices are learned from other horses with the same behavior.

10 feet X 10 feet Stall Grid

Each Square =1 Foot

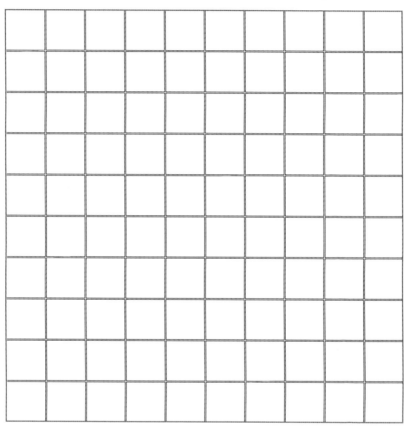

Rein in Language (Journal Writing)

Ready, Set, Write! Write a "How-To" paper for building a new horse shelter. Follow these basic steps to create four paragraphs. Keep it simple; write 3-5 sentences per paragraph and be sure to keep a dictionary and thesaurus handy.

Paragraph #1 - Explain why your horse needs a new shelter and what the shelter will look like.

Paragraph #2 - List materials needed and how you will prepare the building site.

Paragraph #3 - Explain in simple sentences how to construct the shelter using words like first, second, next, and finally.

Paragraph #4 - Finalize your thoughts by writing how and why this shelter will be a safer and more comfortable environment for your horse and reasons why your horse needs a shelter.

Handy Writing Tips:

★ Connect your ideas by restating (repeating) some of your beginning thoughts in your final paragraph. This will help your audience better understand the main idea of your paper.

★ Hold your horses on the title until you've finished writing. This will help you have a better idea about the message you are trying to share.

Did You Know?

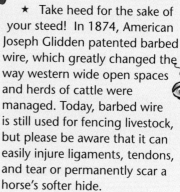

★ You can actually help a stalled horse's mental and physical well-being by giving him or her time to move freely in a turn-out pen, pasture, or arena.

★ Take heed for the sake of your steed! In 1874, American Joseph Glidden patented barbed wire, which greatly changed the way western wide open spaces and herds of cattle were managed. Today, barbed wire is still used for fencing livestock, but please be aware that it can easily injure ligaments, tendons, and tear or permanently scar a horse's softer hide.

Grooming ✕ ✕ ✕ ✕ ✕ ✕ ✕ ✕ ✕ ✕

Besides the basics, like stimulating circulation and teaching ground manners, grooming is also a good time to check your horse's overall health. Grooming not only improves the way a horse looks and feels, it also gives the horse and horseman time to get to know each other and build a lifelong relationship that is so special it is sometimes hard to explain!

PHOTO COURTESY OF AQHA

Horse Lingo

★ *The frog* is the v-shaped pad at the back and underside of the horse's hoof that serves as a natural shock absorber.

★ In England, a *halter* is called a *head collar*.

★ A mane clipped off from the withers up to the poll is called a *hogged* or *roached mane*.

★ The *saddle patch* is the area left unclipped where the saddle sits on a horse's back.

Tools of the Trade

It's important to know the basics about grooming tools and how each tool is used in the grooming routine. Knowledge is power and your horse's good health depends on you learning how to be the best horseman and groomer possible!

Objective: To become aware of basic horse grooming tools and use language skills to work a cross-word puzzle.

Time: 20 minutes

Materials: Tools of the Trade cross-word puzzle

Saddle Up: Explore the following list of basic grooming tools:

1. **body brush** - soft-bristled brush used to remove dust, grease, and light dirt

2. **dandy brush** - hard-bristled brush used to remove dried mud and sweat

3. **mane comb** - long-toothed comb used to detangle mane and tail hairs

4. **curry comb** - rubber comb used to remove sweat and stimulate skin

Keep going!

Hoof Pick   Dandy Brush

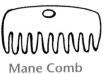

Curry Comb

Mane Comb

5. **hoof pick** - used to clean out hooves

6. **hoof oil**- used to strengthen and shine hooves

7. **shampoo** - used to clean hair and skin

8. **scissors** - used for small trimming projects

9. **towel** - used as a drying cloth to give extra shine to horse's coat

10. **sponges** - used to clean eyes, nose, and mouth

11. **bucket** - used to hold bathing suds or grooming tools

A bit of good horse sense about using grooming tools:

★ Always rinse tools after grooming. Keep tools labeled, organized, and stored in a place that is secure from other animals and protected from the weather.

★ Try to groom outside so that hair and dust won't contaminate water and feed sources.

Now, test your knowledge about basic horse grooming tools by completing the cross-word puzzle on page 78!

Keep going!

Tools of the Trade

Across

1. rubber comb used to remove sweat and stimulate skin
3. hard-bristled brush used to remove dried mud and sweat
5. used to strengthen and shine hooves
6. used as a drying cloth to give extra shine to horse's coat
7. soft-bristled brush used to remove dust, grease, and light dirt
9. used to clean hair and skin
10. used to hold bathing suds or grooming tools

Down

2. long-toothed comb used to detangle mane and tail hairs
4. used for small trimming projects
5. used to clean out hooves
8. used to clean eyes, nose, and mouth

(answers in Appendix)

Trail Talk: Talk about which grooming tools you use the most and why. Then share ways that tools can be labeled and stored.

Ride Further:

★ Keep a good list (inventory) of grooming tools. Make a weekly check to see that tools are not lost or misplaced.

★ Have a fun grooming tool swap session by bringing old, new, or unused grooming supplies to swap with other horsemen.

Imagine that you're a horse!

Barn Talk!

If you were a horse, what kind of grooming techniques would you like the most and the least and why? Think about what your own horse likes best when it comes to grooming.

Hey Horse Pals!

That was fun! Learn more by logging on to **www.JuniorMasterHorseman.com!** Don't forget to ask permission!

Rein in Language (Journal Writing)

Bad timing! Roller, your champion roping horse, just rolled in a puddle of mud. Write about how you are going to get him cleaned up and ready to compete.

Did You Know?

★ Older horses often grow white hairs around their muzzle and face.

★ A horse grooming itself or another horse is the sign of a healthy horse.

Hoof & Teeth Care ✕ ✕ ✕ ✕ ✕ ✕ ✕ ✕

Horsemen and their horses have a lot in common when it comes to their feet and teeth; they both wear shoes to protect their feet, and they both visit the dentist to keep their choppers in working condition. Okay … so they don't wear the same kind of shoes or see the same kind of dentist! But their quality of life does depend on how well these body parts are maintained and kept healthy throughout their lives.

Pretend you're a Dentist!

Barn Talk!

President George Washington had terrible teeth. Many of his dentures (false teeth) were made from hippopotamus, walrus, elephant ivory, elk, cow, and human teeth. Pretend you're a dentist. Write him a letter telling him why his horse could not wear dentures too. Think about how horses use their teeth every day.

FOLD HERE

GLUE HE

CUT HERE

TAPE HERE

Hoof It: Learn About and Label Hoof Parts

Knowing about the hoof, and how to care for this very important part of the horse's body, is another great step toward becoming the best horseman you can be! In the following activity, the horse hoof will be explored and labeled.

Objective: To become aware of and label the parts of the bottom (inferior face) of the horse hoof

Time: 30 minutes

Materials: Bottom of the Horse Hoof graphic (labeled on page 83 and unlabeled on page 84)

Saddle Up: Who would have ever guessed that the parts of a horse's hoof would have names like frog, toe, and quarter, just to name a few? If each hoof is not kept in tip-top shape, even standing can be painful. Remember…no hoof, no horse!

Study hoof part names on the next page. Then find the location of each part on the hoof picture.

Keep going!

Hoof Parts

1. Frog
2. Bar
3. Sole
4. White Line
5. Hoof Wall
6. Bulbs
7. Toe
8. Quarter
9. Heel

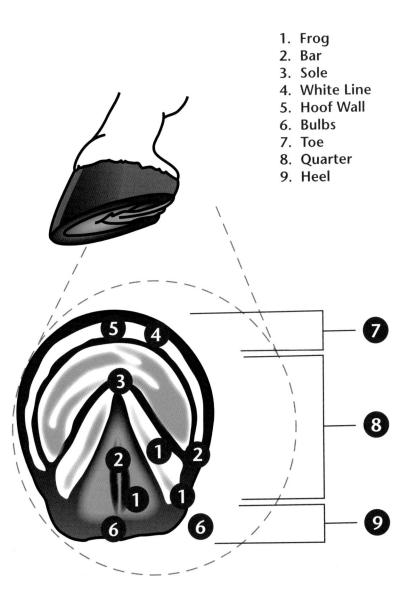

Label the Hoof Parts

Use your new knowledge about hoof parts and label the blank picture with the correct name.

Hoof Parts

1. _____
2. _____
3. _____
4. _____
5. _____
6. _____
7. _____
8. _____
9. _____

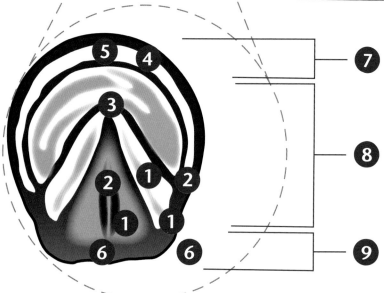

Trail Talk: List other animals that also have hooves. Group the list into single-hoofed and split-hoofed animals. Now, break down those two lists even further by placing one star beside wild animal names and two stars beside domesticated animal names. Note: Domesticated animals are animals that are commonly kept and raised by humans like dogs, cats, and horses.

Ride Further:

★ Take a trip to the local zoo to get a firsthand look at animal feet. Some are webbed or clawed, some are of different hoof types, and some have soft pads for walking.

★ Explore the world of split-hoofed (ruminant) animals like giraffes, cattle, and pigs; they have multiple stomachs!

Horse Lingo

★ Use the term *hoof* when referring to one hoof and *hooves* when referring to more than one hoof.

★ The process of filing a horse's sharp, rough tooth edges with a rasp to create smoother, rounded tooth edges is called *floating*.

★ *Wolf teeth* are sharp teeth in front of the horse's molars, mostly found in male horses.

Foil Horseshoes

What makes a horseman's boots feel just right? It's all in the fit! If the boot isn't the right size and the right type for whatever activity the horseman is doing, it can hurt, cause pain, and bring on a grouchy disposition! Same goes for a horse. When it comes to hooves being trimmed and sized with the right type of horseshoe, the fit needs to be just right. In the following activity, hoof care will be explored and a foil horseshoe will be shaped to fit two differently sized hoof patterns.

Objective: To discover why hoof care is important and practice how good hoof care is important to the horse's overall health

Time: 30 minutes

Materials: Small roll of aluminum foil; scissors; 1 teaspoon per horseman

Saddle Up: Ask horsemen to share their shoe or boot sizes. Inquire if anyone has ever worn a size too small or large. Ask if anyone has ever ran across rough ground barefoot. Invite horsemen to share how wearing the wrong shoe or boot size, or not wearing shoes at all, affects walking, running, or just being comfortable. Read the following information to help horsemen develop a greater understanding of how maintaining a horse's hooves can keep a horse healthy and traveling without discomfort:

Keep going!

Did you know that a horse's hoof is much like a human's fingernail or toenail? It's continuously growing, changing shape, and needs to be manicured and fit for new shoes on a regular basis. If this very important part of the horse's foot is not cared for properly, lameness or permanent crippling can occur. Regular visits by a professional **farrier** (person skilled in trimming and fitting horse shoes) for a filing (rasping) or shoeing can make all the difference.

Different types of horses also have different kinds of hooves. For example, the Thoroughbred has a thinner sole that is likely to bruise much easier than the thicker sole of a heavy draft horse. The type of horse and how a horse is used will often make a difference on what kind of shoes are needed. And if you are wondering how wild horses can go without the attention of a farrier, they usually travel freely enough to keep their hooves naturally worn down.

Now, it's everyone's turn to be a **farrier (FAIR-EE-ERR)**! Use the different hoof patterns on page 89 to properly shape foil horseshoes. If needed, use a spoon to flatten (hammer) the shoe into the perfect shape, just like a farrier would to make the shoe fit just right!

PHOTO BY WYATT McSPADDEN

PHOTO COURTESY OF AQHA

Keep going!

Trail Talk: Talk about the importance of hoof care and how hoof care (good and bad) can make a difference in a horse's overall health.

Ride Further:

★ Observe a professional farrier on the job. Be sure to ask questions, like how long it takes to shoe a horse, where farriers get their supply of horseshoes, and how he or she learned to be a farrier.

★ Paint new or used horseshoes. Add decorations (ribbon, cotton twine, bandana bows, etc.).

★ Gather friends to play an old fashioned game of horseshoes.

Rein in Language (Journal Writing)

Your horse, Champ, is losing weight and seems tired. You take one look inside Champ's mouth and think you know what the problem is. Write about Champ's condition, who you will call to help, and what you think will need to be done to get Champ eating and feeling well again.

Horse Shoe Templates

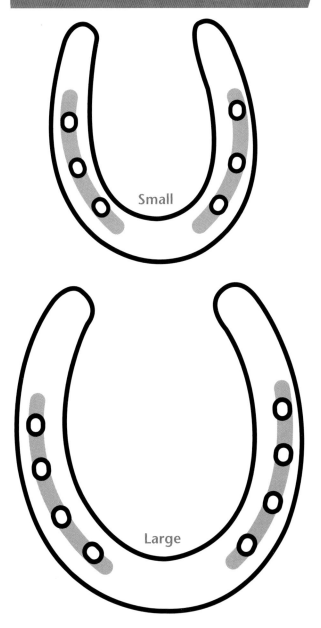

Small

Large

Horse Scramble

What would eating be like without teeth, or with teeth so sharp and jagged that they cut your mouth when you chew? Ouch! You might quit eating, or not eat enough to stay healthy; same goes for your horse. It's very important for you to visit your dentist on a regular basis, but it's also important for your horse to see his dentist, most likely your vet, at least a couple of times a year. Regular checkups can help everyone in the house and around the barn keep a healthy set of choppers and a knock-out smile!

Objective: To use language skills and horse knowledge to solve a word scramble and mystery clue

Time: 15 minutes

Materials: Word scramble

Saddle Up: First, read and solve each clue. Then use the beginning letter from each clue answer to create the mystery horse word and solve the final mystery clue.

Keep going!

Word Scramble

This is a type of horse that is neither light, nor heavy

☐ ___ ___ ___

This is the name used for finding out how old a horse is by looking at his teeth

☐ ___ ___ ___ ___

Leather straps that help control the horse's movement

☐ ___ ___ ___ ___

This kind of horse runs full blast around a track

☐ ___ ___ ___ ___ ___ ___ ___ ___

Injury caused by the hind hoof toe striking the front heel

☐ ___ ___ ___ ___ ___ ___ ___ ___

Faster than a walk, but slower than a run

☐ ___ ___ ___

The hair on the horse's neck

☐ ___ ___ ___

A horse of many, many years

☐ ___ ___ ___

(continued on next page)

Word Scramble *(continued)*

Two letter abbreviation for the country where the American Quarter Horse and Appaloosa breeds originated

⬚ ___

Horse equipment

⬚ ___ ___ ___

Part of the horse that is shoed

⬚ ___ ___ ___

A horse person

⬚ ___ ___ ___ ___ ___ ___ ___

The female parent of a horse

⬚ ___ ___

Final mystery clue:

This is a hyphenated word that describes a horse with an overbite.

___ ___ ___ ___ ___ ___ ─ ___ ___ ___ ___ ___ ___ ___

(See Appendix for answer key)

Trail Talk: Talk about why regular dental checkups are important to a horse's health. Create an emergency veterinarian or horse dentist call list for posting in tack room or office. Most importantly, talk about why it's important for the horseman to have regular dental checkups!

Ride Further:

★ Inquire and compare prices for equine dental procedures such as floating and extracting (pulling) teeth.

★ Interview horsemen to find out how they knew their horse's teeth needed floating.

★ Cooperatively create more word scrambles using familiar horse terms.

Howdy Horsemen!

Don't forget to wrangle your parents up to the computer and register at **www.JuniorMasterHorseman.com!**

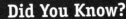

Did You Know?

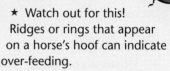

★ The frog of the horse's foot plays a major role in providing a padded cushion.

★ Watch out for this! Ridges or rings that appear on a horse's hoof can indicate over-feeding.

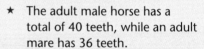

★ The horse's top jaw is wider than its lower jaw. This difference can cause sharp edges to develop that require the teeth to be floated.

★ The adult male horse has a total of 40 teeth, while an adult mare has 36 teeth.

★ If a horse drops a lot of feed on the ground while chewing, this could be a sign that the teeth need floating.

★ A farrier's horse-shoeing forge can reach temperatures up to 2,500 degrees Fahrenheit!

Exercise

Responsible drivers give their vehicle a quick tire, oil, and fuel check before getting out on the road, just to make sure everything is in good running order. Responsible horsemen should also check their ride, just to make sure everything is in good running order, especially before exercising and riding. Exercise is an important part of every horse's daily life. But before you begin exercising your horse, take time to carefully check for soundness and overall health.

Before saddling up, give your horse a good hand check. Feel for any sore spots, bruises, or rough places under the skin. Look closely for cuts that might need doctoring. Cuts on the tongue or chewing on the bit may mean a floating (smoothing of the teeth) is needed. Brush and pick each hoof. Look for eye matting, a runny nose, or excessive slobbering at the mouth. Be aware of your horse's droppings, too, which can alert you to other unseen conditions that can be serious to your horse's well-being. This basic check can help you make good decisions about the type and amount of exercise your horse needs.

DAVID STOECKLEIN PHOTO

PHOTO COURTESY OF AQHA

To Exercise or Not Exercise, That is the Question ... or is it?

How do you feel when you're hungry...grumpy? How do you feel when you can't get outside and play...sad? Did you know that what you eat and how you exercise can affect how you feel and think? Feeding and exercise also can make a difference in how a horse feels and thinks. When there's plenty of feed, water, and room to run and play, a horse will seem satisfied. But cut down on the hay, fresh water, and pen a horse up, and you'll see a big difference...for the worse. In the following activity, the important role of exercise in a horse's life will be explored.

Objective: To better understand the importance of exercise and how activity plays a role in a horse's mental and physical health

Time: 45 minutes

Materials: List for writing physical, emotional, and behavioral effects (below). In other words, how a horse looks, feels, and acts.

Keep going! ➡

Saddle Up: First, let's develop some horse exercise and fitness savvy! Imagine what it would be like to be cooped up in a small area, day in and day out, year after year. What kind of shape would a human be in without sunshine, fresh air, and room to run, play, and exercise? Your skin would probably be pale, your muscles would be soft, your bones brittle, and your disposition could be a little ugly, at best. Horses are no different. They also need sunshine, fresh air, and room to run, play, and exercise in order to keep a healthy body, mind, and spirit. But how much, when, and where, depends on a responsible horseman … and that means you!

You know your horse better than anyone. How would your horse feel if all exercise stopped and he or she could not move around outside of the stall? Use the following activity to write down your thoughts.

Physical effect on the body #1

_____

Physical effect on the body #2

_____

Physical effect on the body #3

_____

Keep going!

Emotional effect (How do you think a horse might feel?)

_____

Behavioral effect (How do you think a horse might behave?)

_____

Trail Talk: Talk about why horses stalled for long periods of time without a regular exercise routine need this type of activity to stay healthy and fit.

Ride Further:

★ Ask a professional trainer to help you develop an exercise routine for your horse(s).

★ Inquire with feed professionals to mix a ration to meet the needs of your horse's daily activities.

★ Visit your local veterinarian to see how injured horses are eased back into an exercise program.

★ Volunteer to help senior or handicapped horsemen exercise their animals on a routine basis.

★ Don't forget, horsemen need plenty of exercise, too. Try power walking to and from the barn. Hoof it as often as you can for your own good health.

Rein in Language (Journal Writing)

Your favorite horse, Blanca, seriously injured her leg getting out of the trailer. The vet says after Blanca is healed, you will need to begin an exercise program to work her back into her normal activities. Write about how you will help Blanca get back into shape and who you will ask for advice on how to accomplish this important task.

Horse Lingo

★ *Laminitis* is a painful foot condition that can also increase respiration rate. It's usually caused by overfeeding or a lack of exercise. This condition can be treated with a restrictive diet, drugs, therapeutic shoeing, and gentle exercise.

★ To *school a horse* means to train it for a specific purpose.

★ The term *pasturing* means just that … keeping a horse in a pasture or open field. Pasturing is important for all horses, especially those stalled year-round.

Horsin' Around with Concho Says!

When a horse is routinely exercised, his or her disposition (attitude) can improve. They also may perform or work with less injury. But best of all, routine exercising can help a horse live an overall healthier, longer life. In the following activity, basic horse movements will be used in fun ways to play and exercise.

Objective: To use listening and gross motor skills to practice basic horse movement and to appreciate the benefits of exercising

Time: 45 minutes

Materials: No materials needed, just a good open human exercise area

Saddle Up: Play Concho's version of Simon Says in an open area where everyone can move about and exercise. Before beginning the game, practice these basic horse movements:

Walk - Natural, slow, even pace.

Trot - Faster than walking. It is a quick and bouncy, two-beat gait.

Keep going!

Canter - Faster than a trot and slower than a run. This is a smooth gait. It is almost like skipping! The front lead leg and same side back leg move together. Western riders call the "canter" gait a lope. When a horse lopes it should carry its head low and relaxed.

Gallop - Fastest gait.

Stop - Sudden or slow complete stop.

Back Up - A slow backward walk after a full stop.

Reverse direction - Horses keep same speed but reverse direction in large circle, always making initial turn toward center of circle.

360 - Full circle turn in place; based on the 360 degrees of a circle.

180 - Same as 360, but only one-half of a circle turn.

Sidepass - From stop position, face forward. Move left or right ("sidepass to the left" or "sidepass to the right"). Important if you're moving to the left, right leg crosses in front of the left, followed by left leg moving in same direction; this is usually done five times. When doing right sidepass, cross over with left leg first.

Include the following movements for extra fun:

Buck - Down on all fours, make a short forward hop on arms before kicking legs high in the air, extending legs as they are kicked out.

Crowhop - A short buck with no leg extensions.

Keep going!

Playing Concho Says

Concho Says can be played as an individual or team effort.

For individual: Encourage horsemen to listen carefully to each basic horse movement command. When the signal is given, check to see that each horseman is correctly modeling movement(s).

For teams: Divide horsemen into small groups. Line up. When the signal is given and the basic horse movement is announced, horsemen (or teams) race each other.

Trail Talk: Talk about why exercise is a healthy habit for humans and horses. List ways that a horse could be exercised, using only a halter and lead rope.

Ride Further:

★ Rate your horse's physical condition as poor, good, or excellent.

★ Set a goal to exercise your horse(s) routinely, no matter what!

★ Chart or record movements you use to exercise your horse and how many times you exercise per week. Be sure to ask an experienced horseman to help you improve or make positive changes to your horse's exercise program.

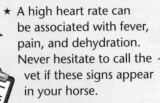

Did You Know?

★ A high heart rate can be associated with fever, pain, and dehydration. Never hesitate to call the vet if these signs appear in your horse.

★ Rushing a horse into exercise after an injury can cause more problems and permanent damage. Be careful to always seek professional advice, and use your own good judgment before allowing a recovering horse to resume normal activities.

★ Gradually ease from a walk to a trot before moving into a gallop. This will allow your horse's body the chance to limber up at a more natural pace.

Be an Inventor!

You've probably heard the saying: Necessity is the mother of all invention. Use your imagination to create a high tech, horse-friendly machine that could improve the way horses of the future are exercised.

Good Job
Junior Master Horseman!

Don't forget to go to
JuniorMasterHorseman.com
to do your comprehension check!

Chapter

4

Health

Vet Care

What's a DVM and why is this person so important to your horse's health? A DVM is a Doctor of Veterinary Medicine. Breeding, foaling, floating teeth, treating wounds, and performing surgery are just a few of the many hats a veterinarian wears when it comes to horses. This highly trained animal doctor will be the person you depend on when you need expert medical advice and your horse needs a doctor's care. Always keep your local vet's phone number in a handy place so you can find it when your horse needs a check-up, or in case there is an unexpected emergency. Your horse's life may depend on it!

PHOTO COURTESY OF AQHA

DAVID STOECKLEIN PHOTO

Imagine the Future

Barn Talk!

Think about how computers and high-tech machines like the X-ray, CAT scan, MRI, and laser have helped doctors diagnose and treat human patients in remarkable ways. Now, let's look ahead to the future: Imagine how new technologies, some not even invented yet, will help tomorrow's doctors treat their two-legged and four-legged patients.

Handy Quick-Check Health Inventory

Objective: To use a simple inventory to determine if a horse needs a veterinarian's care

Time: 15 minutes

Materials: Quick-Check Health Inventory
(*If possible, use the Quick-Check Health Inventory on a real horse.*)

Saddle Up: When you're not sure if your horse needs a vet's care, use the quick-check inventory on the following page. If you check "Yes" on one or more of the following choices, call your local vet immediately!

Don't forget to do Concho's Health Quick Check!

Keep going!

Quick-Check Health Inventory

Head is hanging low and ears will not perk.

Yes _____   No _____

Horse is not eating grain, not grazing, or not drinking water.

Yes _____   No _____

A wound won't clot or stop bleeding, or the horse won't let you get close enough to treat the wound.

Yes _____   No _____

Horse is resting front leg, not moving about freely, or limps when walking.

Yes _____   No _____

Horse is coughing or shows signs of colic (stomach ache) by:

★ **repeatedly lying down and getting up**

★ **frantic rolling**

★ **pawing, kicking, or trying to bite flank**

★ **sweating**

Yes _____   No _____

Eyes are cloudy or matted; gums are not a healthy pink; nose is runny with yellow mucus.

Yes _____   No _____

Keep going!

Trail Talk: Talk about other reasons to call the vet for advice and information. Discuss how keeping in touch with the local vet might help prevent sickness, especially if horses are traveling to other areas and mixing with other animals.

Ride Further:

★ Be prepared! Always keep extra copies of the Quick-Check Health Inventory handy to use and share with other horsemen.

★ To find a local veterinarian in your area via the Internet, search the following Web sites: American Association of Equine Practitioners at ***www.AAEP.org*** or ***www.myhorsematters.com*** (part of AAEP) and ***www.yourhorseshealth.com.***

Go To The Source!

To find out more about the world of veterinary medicine, check out the American Veterinary Medical Association site at ***www.avma.org***

Rein in Language (Journal Writing)

Write about a funny, scary, or amazing experience you have had with an animal. If you haven't had one of these exciting experiences, be creative and make one up!

Horse Lingo

★ *Laceration* is the medical word used to describe a jagged, torn cut that usually needs stitches by a veterinarian.

★ *Moonblindness (uveitis)* is the most common cause of blindness in horses, and is incurable. If you notice swelling, tearing, matting, or anything unusual about your horse's eyes, call the vet in the blink of an eye!

★ A *recoil test* is another name used for pinching the horse's skin to check for dehydration.

The Pinch Test for Dehydration

NOTE: This activity is optional since a live horse is needed to do a check for dehydration.

Dehydration is a condition that humans and animals suffer from when the body doesn't have enough water. Dehydration can be caused by fever or diarrhea. But the most common cause of dehydration is the loss of body fluid from sweating on a hot day or after a hard ride. Some of the more noticeable signs of dehydration for a horse are sunken eyes, red inner eyelids, dry nose, and a drawn flank. So what's a horseman to do? In the following activity, a simple pinch and capillary refill test will be practiced on a live horse.

Objective: To observe and practice simple experiments to check for dehydration

Time: No time frame

Materials: Live horse

Saddle Up: Follow these directions for checking for dehydration:

Gently pull (pinch) the skin from the tissue in the middle of the horse's neck. If a horse is not dehydrated, the skin will

Keep going!

quickly flatten back into place. If the horse is dehydrated, the skin may stay pulled up for around 10 seconds before relaxing. If this happens, the horse may already be in a severe state of dehydration and need attention right away!

Another quick way to check for dehydration is to press your finger into the horse's gum to check capillary refill time. The thumb pressure will keep the blood from the area. As soon as you lift your thumb from the gum, the blood and pink color should quickly return. In a dehydrated horse, the spot you pressed will stay pale and not return to a healthy pink color.

Now that you know what the signs of dehydration are and how you can check your horse for dehydration, what happens next? If your horse is dehydrated, allow him to drink water in small amounts. Electrolytes can be used, but check with your vet before giving your horse anything besides fresh water. Other vital signs, like heart rate and respiration, also should be checked.

DAVID STOECKLEIN PHOTO

PHOTO COURTESY OF AQHA

Keep going!

Trail Talk: The best way to treat dehydration is to not allow it to happen! Talk about ways that you can help your horse get through a hot day or hard workout without getting dehydrated.

Ride Further: The "pinch" test and capillary refill test also can be used on other animals like cattle, dogs, and even humans. With supervision, practice these two checks for dehydration on gentle pets and family members, including yourself, for signs of dehydration.

Did You Know?

★ Nothing scientific about this, but some horsemen think that feeding a horse garlic may help fight worms, respiratory challenges, and keep nasty flies away ... at least the ones that don't like a horse with halitosis (bad breath).

★ Wearing metal horseshoes means a yearly tetanus vaccination is very important!

Prevention ✕ ✕ ✕ ✕ ✕ ✕ ✕ ✕ ✕ ✕ ✕

An ounce of prevention really does go a long way, especially when horsemen are handling, riding, and traveling with horses. Having a first-aid kit handy in the barn and trailer can help a horseman be better prepared in an emergency. The most important thing to remember during any emergency is to stay calm and call for help. Always keep your own safety in mind around an injured horse, or any animal, and do only what you can without jeopardizing yourself and your horse's safety.

Horse Lingo

★ *Proud flesh* is soft flesh bulging from a wound that is not completely healed.

★ *Annual boosters* are yearly shots, like rabies and tetanus, that help protect horses against serious diseases.

★ *Cold therapy* is a treatment used to reduce or help prevent leg swelling and pain.

Important Numbers And Vital Signs

Objective: To better understand how to react in an emergency situation and prepare a list with important emergency information

Time: 30 minutes

Materials: Important Numbers and Vital Signs form

Being prepared is one of the best ways to help yourself and your horse during an emergency! In the following activity, important emergency information will be recorded. But first, think about how the following ideas might help a horseman successfully handle an emergency situation:

★ Call for someone to help YOU first. Then call the vet if your horse needs immediate medical attention.

★ Ease your horse's nerves by talking and acting in a calm manner.

★ If you can't get your horse settled, keep a safe distance away and wait for help.

★ If your horse is down and can't get up on his own, don't try to force him up; wait for help to arrive.

Keep going!

★ If you can safely lead your horse, move him away from any excitement.

★ Give your horse a careful check with your eyes before touching him anywhere. Listen to him breathe. He'll be checking himself out, too, and probably let you know where he's hurting by the way he behaves.

★ Use a first-aid kit for minor wounds that can be safely treated with the help of an experienced horseman. Then you can haul your animal to the vet, or the vet can stop by to give your animal a thorough checkup.

Remember! Keep human and animal emergency numbers and information in a special place near the phone. If you use a cell phone, be sure emergency numbers are entered for quick dialing.

Important Numbers to Keep Handy!

☑ Emergency Number: 911

☑ Phone (Home & Work)

☑ Barn Location/ Address

☑ My Doctor's Name & Number

☑ My Name & Age

☑ Hospital Name & Number

☑ Parents/Guardians

Keep going! ➡

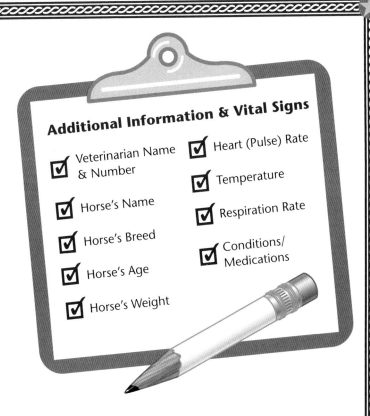

Additional Information & Vital Signs

- ☑ Veterinarian Name & Number
- ☑ Horse's Name
- ☑ Horse's Breed
- ☑ Horse's Age
- ☑ Horse's Weight
- ☑ Heart (Pulse) Rate
- ☑ Temperature
- ☑ Respiration Rate
- ☑ Conditions/ Medications

Trail Ride: Who would be the first person that you would call in an emergency and why? And which person would be next on your list if the first person wasn't available?

Ride Further: Discover more about important horse vital signs and health information by using the *Horse Industry Handbook: A Guide to Equine Care and Management* (American Youth Horse Council).

Preparing an Equine First-Aid Kit

Objective: To review a basic supply checklist and prepare an equine first-aid kit

Time: 45 minutes

Materials: First-Aid Kit list (below)

Saddle Up: It's to the rescue with your homemade first-aid kit! Many of these supplies can be found at the local drugstore. Use a small tackle or tool box, or a plastic tub with a lid to keep your supplies in. Label it with your name and make a cross symbol with red tape so it will be easily recognized. Keep in a safe place away from small children, curious animals, and weather.

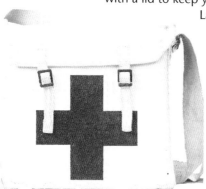

Keep going!

Horseman_____ Date_____

Equine First-Aid Kit Supply Checklist

Yes No   First-aid book for horses

Yes No   Pocket knife; scissors; wire cutters

Yes No   Liniments; antibacterial creams,
sprays, powders

Yes No   Disposable razor
(for shaving hair before treating wound)

Yes No   Rubbing alcohol and cotton balls

Yes No   Wide gauze bandage

Yes No   Adhesive tape; duct tape

Yes No   Vet wrap

Yes No   Syringe (without needle)

Yes No   Thermometer and petroleum jelly
(for checking temperature)

Yes No   Stethoscope (for checking respiration rate
and gut sounds)

Yes No   Other _____

Yes No   Other _____

(Keep this list updated and inside your first-aid kit to help you
remember which supplies need restocking.)

Keep going!

Trail Talk: Talk about how important it is to be ready for an animal emergency around the barn or while at a horse event. Share personal emergencies with animals, both small and large!

Ride Further: Use the following ideas to learn about and practice horse health:

★ Ask experienced horsemen to share experiences and demonstrate how to:

  ★ safely free a horse from tack, like a tangled halter, bridle, or loose saddle

  ★ safely free a horse from fencing or rope

  ★ calm, approach, and pen a runaway horse

  ★ help when a horse is dragging a rider

You're the Vet!

Barn Talk!

You just traveled across three hilly pastures on a hot, humid summer day. Your horse is panting heavily and balks (refuses to move). Think about what might be wrong. What will you do to check your horse's condition and how will you ease your horse's heavy breathing?

FOLD HERE

GLUE HERE

CUT HERE

TAPE HERE

In-a-Fix Horse Emergencies: Role Playing

JMH definition of a FIX: (noun) A fix is a mess or catastrophe; one of those unexpected situations that can happen at any moment. Ever been in a fix? Knowing what to do when you're in a fix, or emergency, is more important than knowing which side of the horse to mount…now that's important! In the following activity, role playing (acting out a situation) will be used to practice safe, common sense ways to handle unexpected horse emergencies.

Objective: To practice problem solving through creative expression and role play

Time: 20 minutes

Materials: In-a-Fix Horse Emergencies (on the next few pages)

Saddle Up: No one expects for an emergency to happen, but they can and they do! Use the following horse emergencies to role play (act out) common sense ways to help each situation:

PHOTO COURTESY OF AQHA

Keep going!

In-a-Fix Horse Emergency

Your gelding, Houdini, has managed to wiggle out of his loose halter and is now standing in the middle of a crowded paddock. He's not moving, but he has that look in his eye. You know, the one that says, "I'm free, I'm feeling frisky, and no one can stop me!" What can you do to keep him from becoming a big problem in the paddock?

In-a-Fix Horse Emergency

Your horse is tied up and you turn on the water hose and accidentally spray a blast of cold water right into your horse's face. This shocks your horse, his back legs slide under him and down he goes! What do you do?

In-a-Fix Horse Emergency

Your filly cut her flank when she playfully ran through a gate patched with rusty wire. The cut is not deep, but it is bleeding. What do you do?

Keep going!

In-a-Fix Possible Solutions

Emergency #1: Call for help; untie the hanging halter, or grab another one and, if the horse will let you, ease the lead over his neck; lure him into an open stall with feed or another horse; allow him to buddy-up with another horse until he settles down and can be caught.

Emergency #2: Stand still and give him a moment to get up on his own; move slowly to loosen or cut the lead rope; call for help if he can't get up on his own or can't get up at all.

Emergency #3: If you can, halter your horse, lead away from the gate area and check the wound; decide if the vet needs to be called (also check to see if there are any more cuts); if the wound isn't serious, get out the first-aid kit and treat the cut; if the wound is bleeding, give it 15 minutes or so to see if it will clot before calling the vet; check vaccination records or call the vet to see if your horse's tetanus shot is current; keep horse away from the gate, and for goodness sake ... fix the gate ASAP (as soon as possible)!

Trail Talk: Talk about how role playing (acting out a situation) with friends helps everyone become better prepared for an emergency, especially a horse emergency!

Ride Further:

★ Create more In-a-Fix horse emergencies. Roll play (act out) three or more possible solutions for each emergency.

★ Name community helpers, like firefighters, police, and paramedics. Talk about why they might also be called to help in a horse emergency, and why they are so important to every community.

★ Why is it important to have an ambulance at a rodeo, race track, cutting, or any other kind of horse event? Arrange for a tour inside an ambulance and discover how paramedics stay ready to help injured horsemen.

Rein in Language (Journal Writing)

You're the trail boss of the annual Mountain Top Trail Ride. Write a letter explaining to riders the importance of packing a first-aid kit. Include a list of supplies and helpful ideas to help riders come prepared and ready for a safe, fun trail ride.

Did You Know?

★ Being in a hot or humid climate, fever, or pain can make a horse's respiration rate go up.

★ Young horses, especially foals, will normally have higher temperature, heart rate (pulse), and respiration than mature horses under the same conditions.

★ The time of day, horse's age, gender (male or female), season of the year, ambient temperature, wind, and barometric pressure can cause a horse's normal body temperature to change.

Pests And Diseases

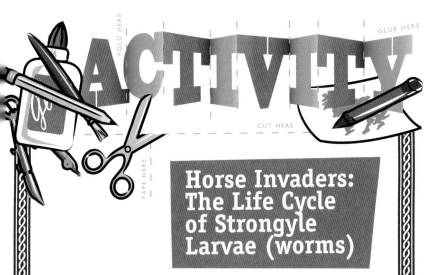

FOLD HERE

GLUE HERE

CUT HERE

TAPE HERE

Horse Invaders: The Life Cycle of Strongyle Larvae (worms)

Did you know that there are more than 150 internal parasites that can harm a horse's health? And what's even worse, these wormy invaders can lay more than 200,000 eggs a day! Parasites can damage a horse's tissue, internal organs, blood vessels, intestines, liver, lungs, and stomach. Some of the signs to watch for are a dull coat, constant rear scratching, and loss of weight. Also know that a horse can be infested with parasites and still look perfectly healthy, so regular deworming treatments are a must! In the following activity, common horse parasites will be named and the life cycle of insect larvae (worms) will be explored.

Objective: To better understand the signs and effects of insect larvae (worms)

Time: 20 minutes

Materials: Life cycle information and comprehension activity

Keep going!

Saddle Up: Understanding the life cycle of insect larvae is an important part of keeping a horse healthy. Parasites are harmful invaders! They can spend up to a year inside a horse's body damaging internal organs. The following parasites are some of the most common found in horses:

★ Large and Small Strongyles (bloodworms) - Found in horses of all ages; divided into two groups: large and small; mostly found in pasture vegetation.

★ Ascarids (roundworms)- Mostly found in foals and young growing horses; hatches in the small intestine, then the larvae travels through the veins to the liver, heart, and lungs; and then back to the small intestine to lay eggs. The life cycle lasts around three months.

★ Pinworms - Less harmful than other parasites; usually found in the rectum and colon; can cause serious irritation around the tail area.

★ Bots (larvae of botflies) - Lay yellowish eggs on legs, throat, and lip hairs. When horse licks hairs, eggs attach to tongue and enter body; develops into an adult fly that looks like a honeybee.

Strongyles (bloodworms)

Keep going!

The life cycle of a Strongyle worm is like a roller coaster ride and goes something like this:

Step 1 - The horse eats and swallows the larvae living in grass, feed, and water.

Step 2 - The larvae lives in the horse's gut or bloodstream until it matures into an adult and lays its eggs.

Step 3 - The eggs leave the horse's body in a manure drop.

Step 4 - The eggs hatch in the manure resting on the ground and the cycle is ready to start all over again!

Keep going!

Horse Lingo

★ *Vaccinations* are shots or doses of medicine that can help prevent and protect animals from harmful diseases.

★ *Influenza (flu)* in horses may also be called shipping fever, and is one of the most common horse and mule diseases.

★ *Gasterophilus* is the scientific name of the botfly.

★ *Encephalitis,* also called Sleeping Sickness, is carried by mosquitoes and is one of the most harmful horse viruses.

Quiz: Life cycle of Strongyle larvae

Use your knowledge about the life cycle of Strongyle larvae (worms) to complete the following sentences.

Fill in the missing words to complete the basic steps of a worm's life cycle:

Step 1

The _____ eats then swallows the _____

_____ living in grass, _____, and water.

Step 2

The _____ lives in the horse's gut or _____

until it matures into an _____ and lays its _____.

Step 3

The _____ leave the horse's body in a _____ drop.

Step 4

The eggs _____ _____ in the manure resting on the

_____ and the _____ is ready to start

all over again!

Keep going!

Trail Talk: Talk about ways that horsemen can take action to prevent parasites:

★ Keep stalls and horse areas extra clean.

★ Feed in an area that is manure-free.

★ Don't keep horses in a crowded area with too many other animals.

★ Allow pastures/pens to rest and naturally rid themselves of parasites.

Ride Further:

★ Take a trip to the local livestock supply store to learn about products used for deworming. Read labels for ingredients, directions, and warnings. Compare product prices. Remember that all medications should only be administered by a vet or experienced horseman!

★ Observe a vet or experienced horseman deworm a horse (or other large animal). Be sure to ask how smaller animals are dewormed and protected from internal parasites.

★ Take a walk around your own horse's area to find sources of insect larvae. Then be a responsible horseman and clean them up!

You Decide!

If you could find a cure for one human and one equine disease, which ones would they be? Why would finding a cure for these diseases be important to you?

Homemade Horsefly Trap

Warning! Warning! Horseflies are thirsty, disease carrying bloodsuckers! These biting insects can carry diseases, like Equine Infectious Anemia (Swamp Fever), from one horse to another. There is no vaccination or cure for this virus, which can be fatal. For a closer look at what's swarming around and biting your horse, make a simple trap. In the following activity, a homemade horsefly trap will be made to collect, identify, and observe horseflies and other insects.

Objective: To use observation skills and written language to better understand parasites

Time: 45 minutes

Materials: 2 liter plastic soda bottles; heavy scissors or kitchen knife; 24" length of string (one per trap); hole punch; bait (moist piece of raw meat or ripened fruit); *(Optional: jar and microscope for observation)*

Saddle Up: Are biting, bloodsucking flies and mosquitoes insects? Yes, they are! So are butterflies, and they look nothing like a fly or mosquito. All insects have three body sections, six legs, two antennae, compound eyes, and a hardened exoskeleton. What makes a fly and mosquito unlike other insects, especially the beautiful

Keep going! ➡️

butterfly, is that they only have two small wings made for speedy flying and sponging or sucking mouthparts that give them the ability to bite and spread infections.

Create your own homemade horsefly trap to collect and study what's swarming around your horse's home by following these steps:

1. Rinse a 2- or 3-liter plastic soda bottle, remove label, cap, and cut the bottle in half.

2. Invert (turn upside down) the top and set inside the bottom half.

3. On opposite sides of the bottle, punch holes. Lace string through the holes. Tie and knot for hanging flytrap.

4. To open and close trap, slide top half up the string. Add fruit or meat for bait.

5. Hang trap in a shaded area, away from children or rodents.

6. Check and empty trap daily and record findings on the Horsefly Trap Observation form on the following page.

String

Top Half
Bottom Half

Bait

Keep going!

Now What? Put flytrap in the refrigerator or ice chest. The cold temperature will not kill the insects but cause them to drop to the bottom of the trap so they can be studied. Use tweezers to quickly separate the flies from other insects. Be careful to not pinch off wings or legs. Keep in mind, there are many species of horse flies, ranging from 3/8 to just over 1 inch long and they may vary in color. Some are all black while many have colored patterns on their abdomens and wings. Record your observations on the form below. After recording your information, dispose of the flies and be sure to wash your hands with soap and warm water.

Horsefly Trap Observation

Flytrap location: _____

1. How many minutes, hours, days, or weeks did the flytrap hang before it was checked?

   Minutes _____ Hours _____ Days _____ Weeks _____

2. What kind of bait was used in flytrap? _____

3. What is the total number of insects in

   the flytrap? _____

4. How many horseflies are in the trap? _____

5. Describe what the horseflies look like? (Number of wings and legs, color, size, etc.) Draw pictures of any flies in the trap. _____

   _____

6. Draw a picture of other creatures in the trap. Name or describe each creature.

7. What did you learn by making the flytrap?

I learned _____

_____

_____

_____

_____

8. What did you learn about insects and horseflies that you

didn't know? I learned _____

_____

_____

Trail Talk: Talk about how a horse acts when he is being bitten by horseflies. (He may throw his head, stamp his feet, bite at himself, kick, seem restless or aggravated, and not be able to graze or drink water).

Ride Further: Find out more about the mosquito and the latest news on West Nile Virus. Find out what horsemen can do to help protect horses from getting this deadly viral infection.

Rein in Language (Journal Writing)

You've just hatched as a brand new horsefly, but you only have three days to live. Write about what you are going to do during your short three-day life? What will you hope to accomplish. before your time is up in the horse pen?

Did You Know?

★ A horse can drop over 25 million parasite eggs per day in its manure: so keep stalls mucked out and horse areas clean!

★ To prevent parasite infection in foals, they should be dewormed at least every two months throughout their first year of life. Most adult horses should be treated for worms every six to eight weeks.

★ An adult ascarid parasite may reach up to 22 inches in length!

★ Stomach bot eggs live on horse hairs. When licked, bots attach to the horse's tongue and can actually cause tongue and gum erosion.

Chapter 5

Nutrition

Nutrition ✕ ✕ ✕ ✕ ✕ ✕ ✕ ✕ ✕ ✕ ✕

Have you heard? Horses need a balanced nutritious diet to grow strong and stay healthy. But how does a horseman know which feeds are best and how much feed a horse needs? A horse's age, condition, activity, metabolism, and even seasonal climate (winter or summer) are all factors

PHOTO COURTESY OF AQHA

that must be considered when feeding. Now, let's get busy learning how to keep that amazing eating, pooping, super equine machine fueled up and ready to run.

✕ ✕ ✕ ✕ ✕ ✕ ✕ ✕ ✕ ✕ ✕ ✕ ✕ ✕ ✕

Horse Lingo

★ *Forages* are the leafy, green plants horses like to graze on, such as grass, hay, and chaff which is chopped hay and straw that is often mixed with molasses.

★ *Colic* is a painful cramping in the horse's intestinal gut.

★ A *flake* is one-tenth of a bale of hay. Ten flakes make a measurement of hay called a bale. Think about this: *Round bales* ARE round cylinders, but *square bales* are not really square, they're rectangular!

Follow the Trail

A horse can easily drink 10-15 gallons of water and eat 20 pounds or more of free-choice hay, plus grain, every day! But don't worry. Eating and drinking this much is perfectly normal for a mature active horse. It's also a must to keep those finicky, fussy horse guts working just right. But that's not the end of this tale, or should we say, tail? A 1,000 pound horse with a healthy diet can drop around 40-50 pounds of manure and release 8-10 pounds of urine every day! Just follow the trail ... there's no doubt that the horse is truly an amazing four-legged eating, pooping machine.

These natural grazers, classified as nonruminant herbivores, need two main ingredients (water and roughage) in their daily diet to keep their sensitive digestive system working smoothly. Horses need to consume (eat) 1-2 percent of their body weight in forage (grass, hay, chaff) every day. The amount of forage that a horse needs per day will depend on activity, condition, and stage of life. This is why free-choice hay or pasture grazing is a daily need for every horse, large or small, active or retired. By the way, did you know that horses even graze during the night?

Keep in mind that good quality hay should be the main part of every horse's diet. Hay also meets nutritional needs and is normally less expensive than mixed feeds.

PHOTO COURTESY OF AQHA

DAVID STOECKLEIN PHOTO

A good feed program provides nutrients from forage and mixed feeds with high energy-producing proteins, fats, and carbohydrates, not to forget important minerals and vitamins. All of these nutrients help a horse grow, perform, and reproduce in a horse-healthy way.

Too little, too much, or poor quality feed can easily upset a horse's digestive system and cause colic, founder, or even obesity (overweight). Poor feeding can also cause a horse to develop vices (bad habits) like chewing wood, also called cribbing. Also, knowing how to feed can make a difference in a horse's health. Placing feed bins so feed can be eaten in a natural grazing position (with feed not any higher than the horse's shoulder) can help prevent respiratory problems.

Feeds And Feeding

Knowing everything you can about feeds and feeding ranks right up there with knowing which end is which on a horse ... and you know what a mess being at the wrong end at the wrong time can be! In the following activity, basic horse nutrition will be explored and new knowledge about basic horse nutrition will be shared.

Objective: To become more aware of basic horse nutrition

Time: 20 minutes

Materials: *Follow the Trail* (on the next page)

Keep going!

Saddle Up: Set down the feed bucket for just a minute and have fun creating a list of new knowledge from "Follow the Trail". (*Tip: Use a highlighter to mark interesting facts and new words or information.*)

Create a list of important things you learned by reading "Follow the Trail". Then share your new knowledge about basic horse nutrition with another horseman.

Things I learned about feeds and feeding from reading Follow the Trail. (make a list below)

> **Trail Talk:** Talk about feeding in general: Where feed is bought; how much feed costs; how many animals are being fed (including pets); and why knowing about feed and feeding is important for anyone responsible for an animal's well-being and health.
>
> **Ride Further:** Take a feed room inventory. Keep a clipboard with a dated list of what kind of feed, including hay, and how much feed is stored. Also, list the names of any top-dressings (vitamins, minerals, and supplements). Each time a new sack is opened or a bale of hay is used, mark the list. Then when it's time to go to the feed store, you can take a quick look on the inventory list to see how much of each feedstuff needs to be replaced.

Stall Feeding

It's true…every horse needs to be fed a nutritious diet to live a long happy life, and for a stalled horse, every bite of feed, ounce of nutrition, and gulp of water depends on the actions of a responsible horseman. Here's a short list of good ideas for feeding a horse:

★ How much hay and grain your horse needs depends on body weight, so know how much your horse weighs. Active working or performance horses and broodmares need at least 2 pounds of hay for every 100 pounds of body weight per day, and 0.5 pounds of grain per 100 pounds of body weight. This means that an active horse weighing 1,000 pounds would need to consume (eat) 20 pounds of hay and 5-10 pounds of grain each day to keep the old engine (digestive tract) running smoothly.

★ What kind of hay and feed your horse likes best is something to observe. Let your horse try small amounts of different kinds of hay (not all at one time) and feed to see what his favorite is, especially before buying in large amounts. Consult your local vet for advice to help avoid making your horse sick.

★ When and how often you feed your horse is key. Feed in equal amounts at the same time each day. Any feed or feeding changes should be made gradually to keep from upsetting the horse's digestive system. Active horses should be fed 4-5 hours before working or performing and about an hour after any type of rigorous activity. Horses should not be kept away from water altogether after a hard workout, but watched carefully and only allowed to take small drinks until cooled down.

★ Where you place feed makes a difference too! Keep feed bins off the ground but lower than the horse's shoulders. This will help your horse eat in a more natural position, which may help prevent respiratory problems caused from feeding too high.

★ Why feed good hay like alfalfa to an active horse? Because it's high in energy, protein, and calcium - nutritious ingredients needed to maintain a healthy coat and keep horse guts working like a charm. Be sure to know when your horse's hay was cut and stored because freshly cut hay (less than six months old) can upset your horse's sensitive digestive system.

All of these good feeding practices can help you keep your YOU KNOW WHO fed in a hearty, healthy way.

Hey Horse Buddies!

Come along with me to **www.JuniorMasterHorseman.com!** Don't forget to ask permission!

Stall Feeding: How, What, When, Where, and Why for You Know Who

In this activity, good ideas for feeding a horse will be listed and a true-false exercise will help check understanding. You will test your knowledge of good feeding practices.

Objective: To demonstrate understanding of good feeding practices and use reading and comprehension skills to answer true-false questions

Time: 20 minutes

Materials: Hay Horse Sense True-False Exercise

Saddle Up: Let's keep this simple and use a healthy heaping of good 'ole horse sense to practice how, what, when, where, and why to do a good job feeding YOU KNOW WHO!

Keep going!

Hay Horse Sense True-False Exercise

Use the information you just learned to answer the following True or False statements.

True or False?
(Write T or F in each bale of hay)

 Your horse's weight isn't important when it comes to feeding.

 It's a good idea to make sure your horse likes his feed before buying a large amount.

 Feed in equal amounts at the same time each day.

 Keep feed bins off the ground but much higher than the horse's shoulders.

 Feed good hay like alfalfa because it is high in energy, protein, and calcium.

Keep going!

PHOTO COURTESY OF AQHA

Trail Talk: Talk about other good feeding practices that a horseman could use before and after feeding time to keep the feed bins clean and feed storage areas organized.

Ride Further:

★ Make a personalized feed label collage. Collect feed sack labels. Glue labels and a picture of you and your horse to a 5 X 7 or 8 X 10 size piece of poster board. Spray with gloss sealer. Frame or mat.

★ Build knowledge on feeding and general horse care by reading: Horses: How to Choose and Care for a Horse by Laura S. Jeffrey; Horse Industry Handbook: A Guide to Equine Care and Management (American Youth Horse Council).

★ Create a feed chart for the feed room. Be sure to include instructions for adding any top-dressings (other feeds or vitamins and minerals, etc.) to feed rations.

★ Make laminated labels for feed barrels/containers if feed is stored outside of the bag. This will help anyone feeding to know exactly what is available and going into the feed bucket.

Be an Inventor!

Knowing how much your horse weighs is the first step in knowing how much to feed. If you could invent a device for weighing your horse without using a traditional weight tape or step-on scales, what would it be named, what would it look like, and how much would it cost?

Horse Cuisine: Horse Healthy Treats

Horses are like kids: they love treats and yummy snacks! Since horses are herbivores (plant eaters), they naturally enjoy plant-based foods like fruits, vegetables, and grains. But they also will eat other foods made from flour, like bread and cake, and even some dairy foods. Many horses also have a sweet tooth and will nibble on jelly beans, peppermint and gummy candies; these super-sweet treats should only be given in very small amounts (two ounces or less).

Keep going! ➜

There are also many foods that are NOT horse-healthy that every horseman needs to know about. Foods and plants to avoid altogether are: tomatoes or potato plants; avocado, cherry and peach pits; mustards; any yard and shrub clippings or tree bark; plants known to be toxic, like hemlock, foxglove, yew, ragwort, and nightshade. For performance horses, absolutely no chocolate, sodas or caffeinated drinks, spices like cinnamon or nutmeg, persimmon, willow leaves, or sassafras. These ingredients can affect a horse's competition drug testing. Know what your horse is grazing or feeding on at all times, especially when you are away from the home pasture or feed bucket.

Objective: To become aware of different plants and foods that can be safely fed to horses and create an original healthy horse treat recipe

Time: 30 minutes

Materials: Ingredients; Original Healthy Horse Treat Recipe; pencil

Saddle Up: Now that you are more aware of healthy foods, and not so healthy foods, that a horse can safely enjoy, make the following recipe to treat your horse. Then have fun creating your own original horse healthy recipe!

PHOTO COURTESY OF AQHA

Keep going!

Healthy Horse Treat Recipe: Apple Ball

Ingredients:

1 large apple

Chopped carrots (small pieces, please!)

Cooking oats (people food)

Cereal bran flakes (crushed)

Molasses

Directions:

Cover carrots, oats, and branflakes with molasses. Core apple. Make small cuts and scoop out enough room to fill the apple with the molasses mixture.

An Original Healthy Horse Treat Recipe

by Junior Master Horseman _____ (Your name)

Recipe Name: _____

Ingredients: _____

_____

Directions (keep it simple): _____

_____

_____

Trail Talk: Talk about how horse treats can be used and the best and safest ways to offer a horse a yummy treat:

Place the treat on a flat hand so the horse will not be able to scoop up any fingers. Wearing a leather work glove will also help, or if the horse is too nippy, place the treat in a bucket.

Ride Further:

★ Have an official JMH horse feed taste test by offering handfuls of different feeds to several horses. Record each horse's response. Name which feed(s) seem to be liked the best. Guess why the horses liked each feed.

★ Make a healthy human treat using the Apple Ball recipe idea. Substitute with granola and molasses or sugared flakes and honey or peanut butter. YUM!

Rein in Language (Journal Writing)

Someone forgot to make sure there was enough feed for tonight's feeding. It's late and the feed store is closed. Explain why there is no feed. Then list ways to keep this from happening again. Oh, and please share what the hungry horse nudging you in the back right now is going to eat for supper.

Did You Know?

★ Grains give horses energy, but hay is best for helping horses produce body heat that they need to stay warm during cold winter months.

★ Obesity in horses can cause heart and respiratory problems.

★ Too much grain, and too little ruffage (hay) in a horse's diet can lump when mixed with the horse's saliva and get everything all stopped up!

★ Overeating, gas, gulping too much cold water, and stress are just some of the things that can cause severe colic in horses.

★ Bran is a natural laxative for horses … and humans.

Water

Horses need a good supply of water to survive. In fact, water is at the top of the list … more important than food, shelter, exercise, and even vitamins and minerals. Water helps everyone's body digest food, absorb valuable nutrients, and remove waste. Water also helps control body temperature and keeps internal organs working.

PHOTO COURTESY OF *AMERICAN QUARTER HORSE JOURNAL*

In most situations, horses should have all the water they can drink to help digest all that good roughage they are eating around the clock. Mature horses can easily drink 10-15 gallons or more a day, depending on their activity level and the climate. For stalled horses, water should be fresh and troughs should be kept clean. For pastured horses, water sources should be plentiful and tested for cleanliness, disease, and excessive mineral content.

Horse Lingo

★ *Dehydration* (loss of too much body fluid) is an unhealthy condition for a horse. Water loss can be caused by sweating, lack of drinking, and diarrhea.

★ A *trace mineral salt block* will help the horse replace electrolytes lost from heavy sweating.

Water Watcher

A horse's water supply needs to be checked every day, not only to make sure there's enough water, but also to make sure the water is clean and fresh. Many things can happen to water over time. It can change and become unfit for animals or humans to drink. One thing that can happen to water is evaporation. Evaporation is part of the water cycle where water turns into a gas and is taken up into the atmosphere. Water also can get dirty. Dust, leaves, and trash can be blown into water containers by the wind. Algae (a green organism) and parasites, like mosquito larvae, can grow in water. Humans don't like dirty water and neither do horses, unless they are very thirsty and have no other source of fresh water.

Objective: To use observation skills and measurement to record water quality and quantity over a period of time

Time: Two-week period with short checks for measuring and recording observations

Materials: Measuring cup; fresh, clean water; Water Watcher Experiment and Observation chart; pencil

Saddle Up: Horses can be finicky eaters and drinkers. It's true: You CAN lead a horse to water but you CAN'T make him drink. Most likely, horses won't drink muddy, polluted, hot, or freezing cold water, so keep water

Keep going!

for your horse just like its supposed to be: clean, plentiful, and fresh. Find out for yourself how water can change over time by using the following chart to record observations for this simple experiment.

★ Using a measuring cup, measure and pour 2 cups of fresh water into a pie pan or a similar flat, shallow container.

★ Record the date and the amount of water in the pan.

★ Place the pan outside where it will not be disturbed for two weeks. For best results, this experiment should be done during warmer times of the year.

★ Record the temperature by touch (cool, cold, warm, hot. Observe how the water looks (clean and clear or dirty and murky). Predict what will happen to the water in a week.

Go back to your pan in a week. Record the date and check the temperature. Notice the amount of water left in the pan. Make a drawing or write about the appearance of the water. Does it still look clean and smell fresh? In two weeks, check the pan again and record your observations.

Keep going!

Water Watcher Experiment and Observations

Date:

Water Source:

Temperature: *(circle)* **Cold   Cool   Warm   Hot**

Amount of water:
(Carefully measure and pour 2 cups of water into a pan.)

Draw a picture and write a description:

- -

1 Week

Date:

Water Source:

Temperature: *(circle)* **Cold   Cool   Warm   Hot**

Amount of water: *(circle)* **More   Less**
(Carefully pour water into measuring cup, measure, and return to pan).

Draw a picture and write a description:

- -

2 Weeks

Date:

Water Source:

Temperature: *(circle)* **Cold   Cool   Warm   Hot**

Amount of water: *(circle)* **More   Less**
(Carefully pour water into measuring cup, measure, and return to pan).

Draw a picture and write a description:

How did the water change each time you checked it? Why?

Why do you think this experiment might be useful to a horseman?

What did you learn from this experiment that will help you care for your horse in a better way?

Trail Talk: Talk about what unclean water looks and smells like. Describe how a horse lets a horseman know that water isn't fit to drink. Then think about how many water sources your horse has to drink from and how often they are cleaned.

Ride Further: Expand your water experiment by collecting other waters (lake, creek, tank, ocean, etc.). Try adding another temperature check using a real thermometer. Use the chart above to compare two other water sources with the first experiment's results. Be sure to place these samples in the same kind of pan and in the same area as the first experiment.

Rein in Language (Journal Writing)

Your champion cutting horse is panting, hot, and cranky after working his heart out in a tough competition. Good news is that you won your first champion cutting buckle. Bad news is that your horse is acting like he doesn't feel well. Write about what you will do to check your horse and how you will care for him. And by the way, congratulations on that win!

Watering the Horse and Horseman

All horses need clean fresh water 24/7! How much water depends on the weather, the horse's age, general health, and level of activity. In the following activity, the amount of water a horse and horseman need each day will be explored and figured in quart and gallon measurements. Planning for a herd's daily water needs also will be figured and recorded.

Objective: To better understand the importance of water and the quantity of water a horse and horseman needs every day to survive

Time: 45 minutes

Materials: Each horseman will need a Daily Drinkers and Water Planner chart and pencil.

Saddle Up: Horses, like humans, need water to stay alive. While an adult horseman needs about two quarts (or one half gallon) of water per day, a horse needs from 10 to 15 gallons per day. Ask: Have you ever heard of a ten-gallon hat? Think of how big a hat would have to be to really hold ten gallons of water! In other words, a horse drinks at least 20 times the water that a person does. If the weather is very warm and the horse has been exercising, it may need to drink 15 gallons or more. Look at the chart on the next page and compare the amounts of water needed by horsemen and horses.

Keep going!

Daily Drinkers

Use the key below to count how many quarts and gallons of water a horse needs to drink each day. *(4 quarts = 1 gallon)*

Quarts _____ **Gallons** _____

Horsemen need much less water to survive than a horse does. Count how many quarts a horseman needs to drink each day.

Quarts: _____ **Gallons:** _____

How many more quarts and gallons does a horse need to drink each day? *(Think subtraction!)*

Quarts: _____ **Gallons:** _____

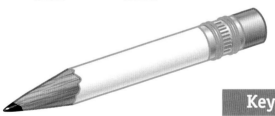

Key

Gallon **Quart**

Now that you know how important water is for a horse to survive, practice figuring out how much water it would take to water 1, 2, 3, 4, 5, or 6 horses. Use the following chart to practice responsible
water planning:

Water Planner

Number of Horses	Gallons each day	Gallons each week (daily amount x 7 days)
1	10	
2		
3		
4		
5		
6		

Trail Talk: Share results of the Water Planner chart. Take new knowledge and the skill of planning water needs even further by figuring how much water would be needed for 20, 50, or 100 horses.

Ride Further:

★ Pour samples of tap water, bottled water, outside hose water, etc., to record how these types of drinking water look, smell, taste, and cost.

★ Use a water testing kit to test barn and house water.

★ Keep a record of how often watering troughs and buckets are cleaned.

★ Check and record average water temperatures during the year at the barn and natural water sources (tanks, creeks, etc.)

An Amazing Body of Water: The Horseman

All living things (humans, animals, and plants) must have water to survive. Have you ever wondered how much water your body is made of? You may find the answer surprising! In the following activity, body weight will be measured and used to find out how much water makes up the human horseman's body.

Objective: To use math skills to discover how much water makes up the horseman's body

Time: 30 minutes

Materials: Bathroom scales; pencil

Saddle Up: First, take a guess: Write down how much water you think your body is made of in pounds. Then follow the steps on the next page to discover the amount of water that makes up your amazing horse-loving body. Record your answers.

Keep going!

Your Amazing Body of Water

1. **Weigh yourself on a scale to find your weight.**

    I weigh _____ pounds.

2. **Multiply your weight by 2.**

    _____ pounds X 2 = _____

3. **Divide that number by 3.**

    _____ divided by 3 = _____

    (This is the amount of water in YOUR body!)

Trail Talk: Was this amount close to the amount you guessed before following the three steps? Name something that weighs about the same as the amount of water in your own body?

Ride Further: While the scales are handy, keep experimenting to measure how much water your horse's water bucket holds. First, weigh an empty water bucket. Then fill it with water and weigh it again. Subtract the weight of the empty bucket from the weight of the filled bucket. How much water did your bucket hold?

Keep going! ➜

Did You Know?

★ Water is an essential
part of the diet needed
for controlling a horse's
body temperature.
  Another way to give a
  horse's natural cooling system
  a kick-start is to gently wet
him down from the legs up.

★ Even though horses cannot
talk, they can communicate.
Some horses let you know
they are out of water by
banging the side of their
horse trough, or they may turn
the trough over.

★ Too much water on a horse's
full stomach can push food out
of the gut before digestion and
cause colic.

★ A hard one-hour workout
can cause a horse to lose
approximately 3 gallons of
water through sweat!

★ Always cool your horse down
before letting him fill up
with water.

Save the Water!

Barn Talk!

There's no if, and, or but about it ... horse's need water every day to survive. If this resource was suddenly cut, how would you make sure your horse had enough water to survive? Think about how to conserve water and plan for future unexpected water shortages.

Vitamins, Minerals, And Supplemental Feeds

Horses need a balanced diet to grow strong and stay healthy. But what type of feed is best for a horse, and how does a horseman know which one to feed? Age, condition, activity level, your horse's metabolism (the way your horse's body processes feed), and climate are all factors that will help you decide which feed(s) to use. For example, the retired bay out in the pasture will have different nutritional needs than the mare and foal stalled in the barn or the futurity champ sprinting down the final stretch. In the following activity, horse feeds will be matched to horse types based on the horse's lifestyle, purpose, or condition.

PHOTO COURTESY OF AQHA

There are many mixes in the feed store made especially for horses that need that extra kick of nourishment to grow, heal, nourish a baby, or perform. Major nutrients needed for a horse to survive and be healthy are water, energy, protein, vitamins, and minerals. Most of these nutrients are found in the feeds' dry matter.

What's Fueling That Feed?

In the following word searches, basic nutrients and ingredients that give feed nutritional value are listed. Have fun searching as a novice or seasoned horseman for scientific words often printed on feed labels (tags).

Objective: To identify and locate feed nutrient and ingredient names in a word search

Time: 30 minutes

Materials: Word Find: What's Fueling That Feed?; highlighter or pencil

Saddle Up: Say the word list. Then find each feed nutrient/ ingredient in the word search! Be sure to mark out each word as it is found.

Keep going!

What's Fueling That Feed?

Novice (easy)

Find These words:

CALCIUM	FAT	FIBER
IODINE	IRON	MINERALS
PROTEIN	SUPPLEMENTS	VITAMINS

What's Fueling That Feed?

Seasoned (advanced)

```
O  M  A  V  O  V  L  L  A  Q  V  D  R  H  P
N  N  U  G  E  M  I  N  Y  I  Z  E  Y  M  H
V  I  W  I  E  G  I  T  T  S  P  T  A  I  O
I  T  E  A  S  M  E  A  A  P  I  G  C  N  S
T  O  C  T  A  S  M  T  O  M  N  N  I  Z  P
A  I  N  T  O  I  A  C  A  E  I  A  E  E  H
M  B  I  B  N  R  U  T  S  B  C  N  A  N  O
I  V  Z  K  T  F  P  I  O  I  L  T  D  I  R
N  R  E  B  I  F  U  D  N  P  A  E  V  M  O
E  V  I  T  A  M  I  N  B  F  E  U  O  A  U
M  I  L  K  P  R  O  D  U  C  T  S  D  I  S
E  S  E  N  A  G  N  A  M  A  C  N  P  H  L
H  B  Y  N  B  M  U  I  C  L  A  C  O  T  G
D  W  S  P  H  W  L  K  D  U  Q  H  I  R  X
M  N  T  Y  U  J  I  O  D  I  N  E  W  T  I
```

Find These words:

BIOTIN	CALCIUM	COPPER	ZINC
FAT	FIBER	IODINE	IRON
LYSINE	MAGNESIUM	MANGANESE	MILKPRODUCTS
NIACIN	PHOSPHOROUS	POTASSIUM	PROTEIN
THIAMINE	VEGETABLE OIL	VITAMIN A	VITAMIN B
VITAMIN D	VITAMIN E	VITAMIN K	

Trail Talk: Make a list of extra supplements (vitamins and minerals) that are fed and talk about how they help your horse feel, heal, or perform better. Name people that would be good to call for advice on putting anything extra into your horse's feed.

Ride Further:

★ Compare horse vitamin labels to horseman vitamin labels. List how they are alike and different. Also, compare costs and directions for use.

★ Find out how fast vitamins dissolve (break up) in water by dropping vitamin(s) into a glass of water. Observe how long it takes for each vitamin to dissolve. This will tell you which vitamins may be absorbed better during digestion. Note: The faster the vitamin dissolves, the better.

★ Read more about vitamins, minerals, and feed supplements in the *Horse Industry Handbook: A Guide to Equine Care and Management* (American Youth Horse Council)

Sell! Sell! Sell!

Barn Talk!

You just created a new supplement guaranteed to give performance horses more zip and vigor than ever before.

Think about ways you can convince other horsemen that your product is better than anything else they have bought and fed to their horses. Tip: Get out the Thesaurus to find similar words (synonyms) that will make your product sound amazing compared to others.

One Lick, Two Licks, Three Licks, Four

NOTE: This activity is optional since a live horse is needed to observe.

Horses need a good lick or two of salt (sodium chloride) every day, but why? The reason is horses can lose salt through their sweat or may not be getting enough in their diet. Salt is usually fed free-choice, either loose (from a box) or in a salt block.

Objective: To estimate how long a salt block will last and how much it will cost for a horse or herd

Time: Unlimited

Materials: New salt block

Saddle Up: This is a fun experiment that will take some time, so please be patient! The task will be for you to see how long it takes for your horse(s) to use up a salt block. There's nothing too scientific about it. You'll just need to use your good observation skills to see how long a salt block lasts. Knowing this will help you estimate how many salt blocks might be used in a week, month, or year, and the cost of feeding salt to your horse or herd. Of course, this will depend on the number and type of horse(s) feeding on the salt block.

Keep going!

Trail Talk: Talk about what supplements (vitamins, proteins, minerals, etc.) are being added to feed rations and why. Then talk about what horseman foods you can add to a horse's healthy diet like carrots, apples, granola, etc.

Ride Further:

★ Study the Morrison feeding standards for a more precise breakdown of dry matter, protein, and nutrients needed by horse weight and different horse types.

★ Collect advertisements for horse supplements, vitamins, and minerals to compare costs and how companies use the media (magazines, flyers, brochures, etc.) to promote their products.

Horse Lingo

★ A *feeding ration* is a mixture of grains, hay, and extra supplements. Other synonyms (words meaning the same thing) for ration are: portion, share, allotment, quota, measurement, and allowance.

★ A *balanced diet* is a diet that has all the important nutrients a horse needs to grow, heal, and stay healthy.

★ *Sodium chloride* is the scientific name for common salt.

Rein in Language (Journal Writing)

What person has helped you more than anyone else become a better horseman? Write that person a letter and share with them how much you appreciate their help, wisdom, and friendship.

Did You Know?

★ Most animal species, including horses, are able to make vitamin C in their body tissues, so adding this vitamin into the diet isn't needed. Only humans, monkeys, and guinea pigs lack this ability. Now you know why your horse doesn't need extra vitamin C, and you now know why you do need to eat foods rich in this important vitamin.

★ Calcium and Phosphorous are the minerals that make up most of the horse's skeleton.

★ Most mature workhorses don't require the extra vitamins and minerals like young growing horses, broodmares, and high performance horses.

Good Job
Junior Master Horseman!

**Don't forget to go to
JuniorMasterHorseman.com
to do your comprehension check!**

Performance

Gait ✕ ✕ ✕ ✕ ✕ ✕ ✕ ✕ ✕ ✕ ✕ ✕ ✕

One of the greatest things about owning a horse is saddling up and riding! Horses are very coordinated and move in rhythmic steps called a gait. Whether riding for pleasure, work, or competition, it's important to know the basic horse gaits: walk; trot (English riding) or jog (Western riding); canter (lope); gallop (run); back (reverse). Each gait has a clear rhythm and pace that gives the rider the pleasure of moving along at ease or blazing a trail at lightening speed.

PHOTO COURTESY OF TENNESSE WALKING HORSE ASSN.

Diagraming a Horse's Walk

First Beat: Right Hind Leg

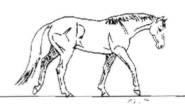

Second Beat: Right Front Leg

Third Beat: Left Hind Leg

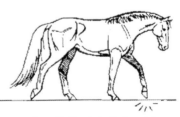

Fourth Beat: Left Front Leg

Let's learn the names and descriptions of the basic horse gaits:

★ **Walk** - In this 4-beat gait, the rhythm of each foot can be easily heard. The walk is a natural, easy pace with a slow clip-clop-clip-clop sound.

★ **Trot (English) or Jog (Western)** - In this 2-beat gait, the rhythm of this bouncy pace is slightly faster than the walk. The feet move in diagonal pairs with the front left and back right moving together and then changing to the front right and back left. The trot, or jog, makes a clip-clop, clip-clop sound.

★ **Canter (English) or Lope (Western)** - In this 3-beat gait, the rhythm of a skipping, or rocking-horse movement, actually lifts all four of the horse's feet completely off the ground at the same time.

★ **Gallop** - Faster than the canter, the gallop is a thunderous roll of all four feet moving at a fast pace.

★ **Back** - Also called reverse, this is a slower backing motion.

FOLD HERE
GLUE HERE
CUT HERE
TAPE HERE

Rhythm of the Gaits

A horse's gait has a clear rhythm and movement; you can feel it! In this activity, horsemen will work together to model gait movements and rhythms.

Objective: To recognize and cooperatively model basic gaits of the horse

Keep going!

Time: 30 minutes

Materials: 4 soda cans for hooves (emptied, cleaned, and crushed); names and descriptions of basic horse gaits

Saddle Up: Grab a partner and four crushed soda cans (two hooves per horseman). Decide which partner will be in front. Work with your partner to model each gait. Be sure to use your sense of hearing to listen for clear patterns of rhythm that clearly define each gait. Experience friendly competition by challenging other horsemen to model basic horse gaits, and please don't forget to recycle the soda cans when you are finished!

Trail Talk: See if you can remember the basic horse gaits. Then share which gaits are used for performance events such as jumping, cutting, and reining.

Ride Further:

★ Invite an experienced horseman to demonstrate how the body, voice, and riding tack can be used to control a horse's gait.

★ Make a video or still photo presentation showing the basic horse gaits using other riding friends.

Hey There!

Don't miss out on more horse fun at **www.JuniorMasterHorseman.com!** Don't forget to ask permission!

Fill In the Gait

Now that you know the basic horse gaits, step on out and put your new knowledge to work!

Read the following situations that a horse and rider could experience. Then fill in each blank with the gait that would be the best choice for each situation.

Fill the blank with the correct Gait:
Walk, Trot or Jog, Canter or Lope, Gallop, Back

1. You're rounding the last turn in a qualifying race.

   Gait: _____

2. You're warming up your horse for a jackpot roping. After walking the arena a couple of times, you break into the next gait.

   Gait: _____

3. You are exercising your horse for a championship barrel race.

   Gait: _____

4. You are leading a trail ride, traveling horseback on rocky, uneven ground.

   Gait: _____

Keep going!

5. You are warming up for a Western Pleasure class. Which gait will you use to check your horse's lead *(the foot used to step out and move the horse forward in the canter or lope)*?

Gait: _____

6. Your horse senses danger. No wonder! There's a snake's den close by and you need to calmly ease your horse away.

Gait: _____

Note: The gait choices you make may differ from someone else's, and that's okay. Talk about your choices and learn why you chose different gaits for each situation.

Trail Talk: Talk about why it is important to learn basic horse gaits. Find out how many horsemen practice unique maneuvers like the sidepass (side movement) and leg yield (diagonal: side and forward movement).

Ride Further: Learn more about the basic gaits and how to improve riding skills:

★ Invite an experienced horseman, and his or her mount, to demonstrate and share ideas about different horse gaits.

PHOTO COURTESY OF PALAMINO HORSE BREEDERS OF AMERICA

PHOTO BY JEFF KIRKBRIDE

PHOTO COURTESY OF USPC

Are we there yet?

It's a four-day drive to reach a world-class jumping competition. Tell how you will care for your horse while traveling to and from the competition.

Horse Lingo

★ The equestrian term *dressage* comes from the French word *dresser*, meaning to train.

★ When someone talks about a horse being *green*, that just means that the horse is still not fully broke or trained.

★ An *extended gallop* is a very fast gait around 16 miles per hour.

★ A *sidepass* is like a side step. In this step the horse's front right crosses over the front left when going to the left, moving the horse across an area sideways. When going to the right, the front left crosses over the right.

PHOTO COURTESY OF AQHA

DAVID STOECKLEIN PHOTO

The Gallop Group Game

It's easy to see how humans walk or run on foot: they just move one foot after the other. But the way horses, or other four-legged animals, move on all four feet with such grace and timing is amazing, to say the least! In this activity, horsemen will work as an individual, then as a team, to experience how a horse gallops and changes leads.

Objective: To experience and identify the galloping gait of a horse

Time: 30 minutes

Materials: Gallop Group Game

Saddle Up: With a horseman leading or riding a horse, watch how easily the horse moves all four legs with such perfect timing and coordination. Which foot is normally used to step out when the horse begins to move? This foot is called the lead, which makes sense since it is the leader, or first one to step out. Okay, put up the horse for now. It's time to think about the horseman's way of moving on foot.

For a horseman to move in a walking or running motion, one foot also has to be placed after the other with rhythm. To demonstrate what a lead foot is, line everyone up and take one step forward. The foot used to step forward is most likely the natural lead foot.

Keep going!

Now that everyone knows which foot is their lead, then it's time to experience a faster gait. The canter is best described as a rocking-horse motion. To experience the human version, or two-legged canter, move forward placing one foot behind the other in a skipping motion. Canter clockwise around a make-believe arena using the right foot as lead. Then circle around and change leads to canter counterclockwise (left). Good job!

Now it's time to try moving with the timing and coordination of a real horse in a group game!

★   Pair horsemen: one will move as the horse's front legs and the other will move as the horse's back legs. Make sure each horseman knows the correct lead foot to start on to gallop to the right and then to change leads and gallop to the left. Have fun giving horses commands, change partners, and keep galloping!

Trail Talk: Talk about how galloping can be the most exciting AND dangerous gait, especially for a novice (inexperienced) rider. Remember, saddle stirrups should always be short enough to keep weight forward so the rider can balance and easily get up out of the saddle.

Ride Further:

★   Search the classifieds in the newspaper or equine magazines to read about horses for sale. Mark each ad with N for novice rider (inexperienced) or S for seasoned rider (experienced).

★   Invite a seasoned (experienced) horseman to demonstrate how the reins and rider's leg pressure can be used to cue (signal) a horse to get on the correct lead.

Rein in Language (Journal Writing)

If you trained horses for a living, what breed or type of horse would you choose to work with? Write about your life training horses and illustrate your thoughts.

Did You Know?

★ Race horses can move around 45 miles per hour in a graceful super-speedy galloping gait.

★ Mexico's modern horse breed, Azteca, developed in 1972, has long, strong legs, an elegant head, and is often used in dressage competitions.

★ Lunging a horse in a circle is a great form of training and exercise.

Tack And Equipment ✕ ✕ ✕ ✕ ✕ ✕ ✕

There's nothing like the good leathery smell of a new saddle! Whether your saddle is brand new, a hand-me-down, or one that came with your horse, it's one of the most basic and important pieces of tack. But there's more! Riding horsemen also need a halter and lead rope, bridle, bit, reins, and saddle-blankets. There's also all of the basic equipment needed to haul, groom, show, feed, and care for a horse. No doubt, being a horseman is a big responsibility, but worth every bit of time, effort, and money needed to enjoy the companionship of a good horse.

Check Your Tack

Let's take a look at these basic pieces of tack:

★ **Riding clothes** - These include boots, pants, hat or helmet, gloves, chaps … anything that helps a horseman ride with safety and protection.

★ **Saddle** (Circle one or both of these common saddle styles - English or Western) A saddle needs to fit the rider, horse, and type of riding it will be used for. It is usually the most expensive piece of tack and can be made in many different styles and with unique design.

★ **Halter, bridle and bit** - Needed to control movement. These pieces should fit the horse's head size and match your type of riding.

★ **Leg wraps** (leggings or support boots) - These help protect the horse's lower legs from getting cut or bruised, and it supports tendons and ligaments that might be overworked or strained.

... and no horseman needs to be without these basic pieces of equipment:

★ access to a trailer

★ grooming supplies (including brushes and extra water hoses)

★ seasonal supplies like fitted blankets and fly/parasite protection

★ clean-up (mucking) supplies for the barn and stall

★ feed pans, water buckets, hay nets

There are many places that basic tack and equipment can be bought like the local tack store, horse events, equine supply magazines, and the Internet. One important key to keeping your tack in good shape so it will last is to store it in a dry place, away from animals like horses, cattle, mules, goats, and dogs that like to lick and chew on leather!

Horse Lingo

★ The *tree* is the skeleton of the saddle that the padding and leather covers.

★ The side flaps of the Western saddle are called *fenders* which are pieces of leather that attach the stirrups to the tree of the saddle. The part you sit on is called the *seat*. Sounds like the western saddle has some things in common with a pickup truck, huh? But that's not all ... it also has a *horn*.

★ A *Youth exhibitor* is a horseman 18 years of age or younger as of January 1 of the current year.

★ A *performance class* is an event where the horse or the exhibitor is judge based on their actions or skills.

Saddle Up, Partner!

The saddle is a horseman's most expensive and exciting piece of tack! There are saddles for every type of riding and event imaginable. Let's take a look at the two most common saddle styles, Western and English. In the following activity, Western and English saddle parts will be named and compared.

Objective: To name and compare the parts of Western and English saddles.

Time: 20 minutes

Materials: Saddle graphics; circle graph; pencil

Saddle Up: Review every part of the Western and English saddle, and compare the parts of each saddle that are the same or different. Here's how: First, list the parts of the Western saddle in the left circle. Now do the same for the English saddle on the right circle. Look at each list and circle the parts that have the same name. List those names in the middle section of the two circles. Now, you can easily see that parts of each saddle may look different, but have alike names. Interesting!

Keep going!

The Western Saddle

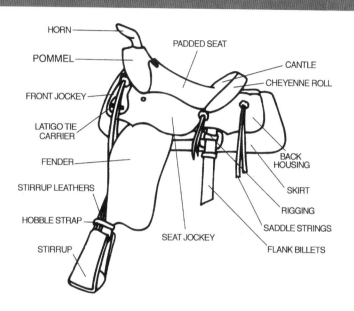

HORN
PADDED SEAT
POMMEL
CANTLE
CHEYENNE ROLL
FRONT JOCKEY
LATIGO TIE CARRIER
FENDER
STIRRUP LEATHERS
HOBBLE STRAP
STIRRUP
SEAT JOCKEY
BACK HOUSING
SKIRT
RIGGING
SADDLE STRINGS
FLANK BILLETS

The English Saddle

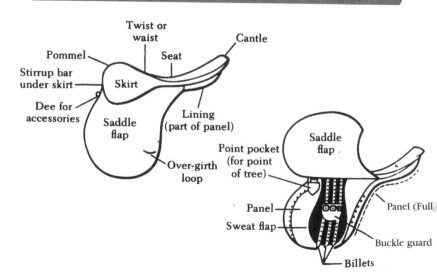

Twist or waist
Cantle
Pommel
Seat
Stirrup bar under skirt
Skirt
Dee for accessories
Lining (part of panel)
Saddle flap
Point pocket (for point of tree)
Saddle flap
Over-girth loop
Panel
Panel (Full
Sweat flap
Buckle guard
Billets

Western   English

Common
Parts

Other types of saddles are made for special events like racing, jumping, hacking, hunting, schooling, dressage, and riding side-saddle! Each type of saddle has special characteristics like weight, shape, and size that help the rider ride with balance and control.

Keep going!

Chapter 6: Performance

Trail Talk: Share ideas about why an English saddle would not work well for a roper, or why a Western saddle would not work well for a jockey or the horse he is riding?

PHOTO COURTESY OF AQHA

PHOTO COURTESY OF AQHA

DAVID STOECKLEIN PHOTO

Ride Further: Saddle up to these good books about horses in general, including horse tack and equipment, by reading:

★ *The Horse Industry Handbook: A Guide to Equine Care and Management* (American Youth Horse Council)

Barn Talk!

Design Your Own Saddle!

If you could design a saddle, what would it look like and what kind of modern-day gadgets would you put on your saddle that saddles don't have today? Draw a picture of your new saddle design. How much will it cost and how long will it take you to make each one that might be ordered? And oh, don't forget to name your new saddle.

Performance Events

Horses are awesome performers! They can do so many things. Here are a few popular performance events:

Western Pleasure - This is one of the most popular show events. Contestants compete in a class together, traveling the perimeter (outer edge) of the arena. A judge standing in the arena's center will ask the class to walk, jog, lope, and reverse (change direction). The judge may also ask the horses to stop at any time. The horseman must ride and carefully follow the judge's directions at the same time. Horses are evaluated (judged, scored) on quality of movement while staying quiet and calm, and soundly traveling with ease on a loose rein.

Barrel Racing - An exciting race against the clock in which the rider runs a triangular (clover leaf) pattern made with three barrels. Riders choose to circle either the right or left barrel first, race to the opposite barrel, and complete the course after circling the third barrel at the far center of the arena. The rider and horse then run full-speed racing through the center of the pattern and out of the arena to stop the timer. Knocking over a barrel carries a five-second penalty.

Pole Bending - A timed event in which the speed and agility (skill) of the horse are tested as horse and rider weave through a course of six poles spaced 21 feet apart. The pattern takes the rider to the far pole to then weave in and out of the poles down the pattern and back up before turning around the far pole and running full-speed to exit the arena and stop the timer. The pattern must be followed exactly and a five-second penalty will be added for each pole knocked down.

The Imaginary Arena: Performance Fun

Who needs a real horse to ride western pleasure, or blaze a trail running the barrels or poles? Not a creative horseman with an imaginary horse and arena, that's who! In the following activity, event knowledge, skill, speed, and imagination will take you around the arena to perform in western pleasure, barrels, and pole bending.

Objective: To use gross motor, directional, and cooperative learning skills to perform different performance events

Time: 15-45 minutes

Materials: Western pleasure, barrel racing, and pole bending descriptions and patterns; judge (extra horseman); stop watch; optional: hat, boots, whip, spurs, and awards.

Saddle Up: Find a space that you can run and play in like a large room, playground, or an area outside free from objects that might get in the way for a moving horseman. After reading each event description, mount up on your imaginary horse to ride in each one of the following popular and fun events. Good luck!

Tips before you begin:

Western Pleasure: Select a judge, or be your own judge. Call out the commands and perform

Keep going! →

your very best. If you have an extra horseman handy, add another judge for showmanship.

Barrel Racing and Pole Bending: Use ordinary objects like stools, feed buckets, pillows, etc. (or cones if you have some) to set up these speedy timed event patterns.

> **Note from the author:** *As a youngster, when I was away from my American Quarter Horse, Red, or if bad weather kept me inside, I would spend hours and hours practicing these events and running these patterns. There's no telling how many World Championships I won in my imaginary arena! It was a simple kind of fun - the kind of fun that still brings me great joy when I think back on those wonderful, exciting days in the saddle.*

> Trail Talk: Share thoughts about competing in the imaginary arena events. Then share real life experiences in the arena! In a real arena, which of the three events are the most physically stressful for a horse. Also talk about the best ways to warm-up and exercise before riding in any arena event.

Ride Further: Never stop learning new things about the fascinating world of horses! Discover more about showing and riding by using these ideas:

★ Tune in to America's Horse. This great family-oriented television program, produced by the American Quarter Horse Association, is packed with all kinds of useful and interesting information for all horsemen, young and old! To find out more, visit the American Quarter Horse site at **www.aqha.com**.

★ Visit the National Reining Horse Association at **www.nrha.com** to find out more about this judged event that showcases the athletic ability of a stock-type horse in a show arena.

A Bit about Head Gear

The bridle, bit, and reins are the main pieces of tack that make up a horse's headgear. These pieces of leather and metal all work together to help the horseman control and guide the horse. In the following activity, the two main types of bit, snaffle and curb, will be explored. How to measure a horse's mouth and how to fit a horse's mouth with a bit will be practiced.

PHOTO COURTESY OF AQHA

Objective: To practice measuring a horse for the correct size of bit

Time: 15 minutes

Materials: New pencil; 12 inches of string; ruler or tape measure; Optional: Live horse

Saddle Up: Here's a bit of interesting information: Did you know that before metal was used to make bits, they were made of wood and bone? Today there are many styles of bits made from rubber, copper, and nickel, but many horsemen like to ride with a iron bit. Look at the following information on the two main types of bits, snaffle and curb.

Keep going!

The main difference between the snaffle and curb bit is that the curb bit has shanks.

Snaffle Bit: This bit is a milder bit than the curb bit. It is a thick bit, usually jointed in the middle. The snaffle bit puts pressure on the horse's lips, tongue and bars of the mouth.

Curb Bit: This bit can be more severe on the horse's mouth. Curb bits have a curb chain, which fits under the horse's chin and helps to lower the horse's head when the reins are pulled. This bit puts pressure on the horse's tongue, bars of the mouth, and the poll.

So how does a horseman know how to fit a bit to a horse's mouth? Let's practice on ourselves or another horseman first. Then measuring a horse for a bit will be even easier!

Here's how: Tie a string to the middle section of a new pencil. Lay the string across the tongue from one corner of the mouth to the other. Pull the loose end (the end opposite the pencil) until the pencil catches on the opposite side of the mouth. Mark the string. Remove string and measure in inches to find the width of the mouth.

How wide would your bit, or another horseman's bit, need to be in inches? _____inches

For measuring a real horse for a bit, follow the same steps with supervision from an experienced horseman. And just so you'll know a bit more information in your back pocket when you look at bits: Most horse's mouths are about 5 inches wide. Here are some guidelines from the AQHA Official Handbook-(2006).

Trail Talk: Talk about commands that can be given to a horse by using the bit. Find out which bits other horsemen use when riding.

Keep going!

ACCEPTABLE CHAIN CHIN STRAPS

WESTERN BITS

LEGAL BIT

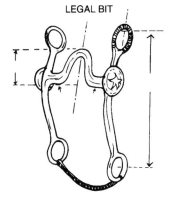

ILLEGAL BITS

DONUT BIT   PRONG BIT

Keep going!

Acceptable English Bits
For All Ages

SLOW TWIST

CORKSCREW

DOUBLE TWISTED WIRE

SINGLE TWISTED WIRE

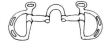

CORRECTION BIT

SNAFFLE BIT WITH CONNECTING FLAT BAR

Unacceptable English Bits

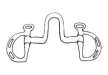

EXCESSIVE PORT

TRIANGULAR MOUTH

Keep going!

Ride Further:

★ Start a collection of bits. Find out as much information as you can about each bit's history.

★ Find out which weighs the most: a bit or a horse shoe?

★ Compare bits by having a fun show and tell, or trace around bits to compare size and shape of different bits.

★ Cut out pictures of bits in advertisements to see how many different bit styles you can find. You might be amazed!

★ Bits make interesting decorations. Sew a light bit on a pillow, or trim the Christmas tree with a bit here and there to add a creative, fun, and genuine horse theme!

Rein in Language (Journal Writing)

Which event is your favorite? Write a short description telling how the event is performed. Be sure to tell your reader what kind of equipment is used and if your event is timed or judged. If you've never ridden in an event, then use one of the event descriptions from the Imaginary Arena activity and have a go at making your readers believe that you're an old pro!

Did You Know?

★ Be aware that leather will darken when cleaned with wax-based products.

★ Good quality leather has a warm inviting smell. Poor quality leather may smell fishy ... eeewww!

★ A saddle that doesn't fit the rider just right can cause bruises and be uncomfortable. The best way to prevent this is to test drive the new saddle to make sure it's a good fit on you and your horse!

★ When riding alongside the road or in public areas, it's always a good idea to wear reflective or bright clothing so motorists can see you and your horse.

What Horses Do ✕ ✕ ✕ ✕ ✕ ✕ ✕ ✕ ✕

What **do** horses do? Horses are used and enjoyed in many different ways. Some horses compete in events, do basic work, or are only used in breeding programs. Others are used for pleasure, and then there are those special horses that serve in a therapeutic way, helping people heal or rehabilitate. One thing's for sure, horses are one of the most useful and helpful animal species on the planet. And like Winston Churchill once said, **"There's something about the outside of a horse that is good for the inside of a man."**

✕ ✕ ✕ ✕ ✕ ✕ ✕ ✕ ✕ ✕ ✕ ✕ ✕ ✕ ✕

Barn Talk!

You Win!

Imagine this: YOU … YES, YOU just won an event at the World Competition. Share how you and your horse accomplished this big goal and what other horsemen need to know about competing on this level.

Puzzling Pictures

Riding and competing in events with your horse is one of the most fun experiences in the world! In the following activity, pictures of different events will be colored, cut up, and puzzled (pieced) back together.

Objective: To use visual and memory skills to name, color, and cut. Then puzzle (piece) pictures of horses and riders participating in different events

Time: 15 minutes

Materials: Puzzling Pictures (on the pages following this activity — pages 199 thru 201); colors; scissors

Saddle Up: Name and discuss the events that each picture represents. Color each page. Cut each page into puzzle-like pieces: not too small and not too large! Mix up the pieces and then put them back together as fast as you can. If you need, number or name each event picture on the back of each piece. For younger horsemen, puzzle together one page at a time, then move onto working with multiple pages at once ... a fun challenge that can be played alone or with friends.

Keep going!

Trail Talk: Name every horse event that you can think of. Talk about each event and share ideas about which events you think are the most fun and challenging. Talk about special skills and training needed for each event.

Ride Further:

★ Watch a performance event that you would like to learn more about.

★ Before you begin a new event, read about it, talk to others about it and decide why it might be a great competition event for you and your horse.

Horse Lingo

★ The term, *Gymkhana*, comes from the East Indian word meaning games on horseback. Barrel racing and pole bending are both considered gymkhana events.

★ When a judge *pins a class*, he or she is selecting the top group out of the class, and the winner or champion will be picked out of this group.

★ A *go-round* is a preliminary competition that qualifies a competitor for finals in an event.

★ A *furlong* is a unit of distance equal to 220 yards (200 meters). There are 8 furlongs in a mile.

DAVID STOECKLEIN PHOTOS

PHOTOS COURTESY OF AQHA

Rate-a-Horse

Before you decide which events your horse would be best at, or how you will enjoy your horse, it might be a good idea to rate your horse's characteristics, including personality and abilities. This survey also can be used before buying a horse to give you a better idea of what kind of gent (gelding or stallion) or lady (mare) you are thinking about taking home.

Objective: To use a simple survey to rate horse characteristics

Materials: Rate-a Horse Survey; pencil

Time: 15 minutes

Saddle Up: Okay, this is just ONE more way to get to know your horse better, or to begin getting to know a new horse better. Read each characteristic and circle your choice of answers to see how your horse's characteristics rate. If you don't have a horse, then answer the survey with your dream horse in mind!

Keep going!

Rate-a-Horse Survey

Friend or Foe? My horse is...

a. affectionate and enjoys grooming

b. uneasy about being touched by anyone

c. unsociable, unfriendly

Excitability

a. easy going, calm

b. jumpy, tense, easily spooked

c. prances, pulls away, high-headed and wide-eyed, runs away

Disposition

a. gentle, friendly, at ease

b. curious, can be caught with feed, semi-friendly

c. unsure of humans, hard to catch, unfriendly, touchy

Spirit

a. dead-head, lazy

b. full of energy but easily controlled

c. high-spirited, dangerous to others, unpredictable

Keep going!

Sensitivity

a. slow to go

b. responds well to commands like "easy now", and "whoa"

c. likely to get away and run, hard to control

Tolerance

a. gentle, trustworthy, good-natured

b. likes most horses, sometimes unpredictable

c. moody, unsettled, a challenge to be around

List how many a's, b's, and c's you circled for your horse. The letter with the greatest number should describe your horse.

a _____ Your horse is good-natured and should be ready to perform and be used in many ways.

b _____ Your horse is energetic and ready to be trained for competition, basic work, and pleasure riding.

c _____ Your horse is high-spirited, unpredictable, and could benefit from working with an experienced horseman or trainer.

What did you learn about your horse (or another horse) from this survey?

I learned that my horse _____

_____

_____

_____   **Keep going!**

Trail Talk: Talk about other ways a horseman can get to know his/her horse better (grooming, riding, interviewing past owner(s), etc.).

Ride Further: Spend time getting to know your horse better by using these ideas:

★ Go on an organized trail ride.

★ Attend a horse camp to learn more about riding, grooming, and competing.

★ Ride in local events and parades.

★ Join a riding club or association

★ Spend time around others that are learning about horses.

Rein in Language (Journal Writing)

You are on the hunt for a new performance horse. You decide to put an ad in a leading equine horse magazine. Write about what kind of horse you need for your event and what characteristics you are looking for in a performance horse. Be sure to include your name and contact information.

The Next Best Thing: The Mop Horse

If you've never made and played with a mop horse, you've been missing out on a lot of fun! The mop horse has been around just about as long as the mop! In the following activity, a simple mop horse will be created and used in a fun way to practice events and riding skills.

Objective: To use some creative imagination to make a mop horse and practice basic horse events, riding patterns, and horsemanship skills

Time: 45 minutes

Materials: Mop (cheap); 4 strong rubber bands; baling twine, long, soft leather strips or a string for bridle and reins (Use your imagination!). Option: Use paint to mark breed characteristics

Keep going! ➡

Step 1:
Take 1/3 of mop

Step 2:
Fold and place rubberbands to create face

Step 4:
Take braids separately and fold for desired ear size and place rubberband to hold

Step 3:
From each side, take three strands and braid

Step 5:
For final touch place brown yarn to create bridle as shown in picture

Saddle Up: Gather up the mop strings in your hand. The first 1/3 of the mop head will be folded under and rubber banded close to the stick (throat area of the horse) to make the length of the head. A second rubber band will be wrapped at the nose. To make ears, pull out three mop strings, rubber band each ear and braid. Ears may need to be shortened, if too long.

Now, mount up and run the barrels, a reining pattern, poles, a jump course, or practice the gaits on your fun mop horse. The ideas are endless. How about a western pleasure class or cutting competition? Kick up the competition by timing everyone and awarding homemade goodies (treats) in place of ribbons and trophies.

Keep going!

Trail Talk: Talk about ways to improve horsemanship skills on and off the horse. Name other horsemen that are experienced and could help teach skills in grooming and riding.

Ride Further:

★ With a group, gather mop horses into breeds or horse types.

★ Have a mock show.

★ Brainstorm about other animals that could be made out of a mop.

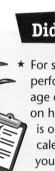

Did You Know?

★ For showing and performance events, the age of a horse is based on how old the horse is on January of each calendar year. How old is your horse based on this rule? In Argentina and Brazil, the date is July. How old is your horse based on this rule in these two South American countries?

★ The fastest horse ever recorded was Big Racket. This speedy horse ran in Mexico City in February 1945 at an amazing 43.26 miles per hour. (Guinness Book of World Records)

Congratulations, First Place Junior Master Horseman!

There's nothing like the thrill of placing in an event and taking a colorful ribbon home to add to the collection. Earning a ribbon or trophy to remind you of all the hard work and fun that you and your horse had competing against others is something mighty special! In the following activity, a first place show ribbon will be made for a job well done for becoming the best horseman you can be and for participating in this exciting Junior Master Horseman project.

Objective: To use fine motor skills and creative expression to create a paper show ribbon

Time: 30 minutes

Materials: Small metal coffee can; pencil; 4 - 8 X 10 pieces of paper (purple or blue); scissors; glue; stick-on letters or marker (white, silver, gold, etc.) for lettering; optional - stapler

 Keep going!

Keep going!

Saddle Up: Look at the twelve show ribbons on the previous page. Did you know that there is a special color for first place through tenth place, Reserve, and Grand Champion? Test your skills on numbering and coloring each ribbon with the correct color. Then check your work by looking at the answer key below.

Answer key for coloring ribbons:
First- blue; Second- red; Third- yellow; Fourth- white; Fifth- pink; Sixth- green; Seventh- purple; Eighth- brown; Ninth- dark gray; Tenth- light blue; Reserve Champion- red, white, and yellow; Grand Champion- blue, red, and yellow.

Now, you're ready to follow these simple steps to make your own Junior Master Horseman first place ribbon:

★ Place the coffee can onto the first piece of blue paper. Trace center pattern and cut out.

★ Fan-fold the second and third pieces of blue paper into inch strips, starting at the top of the paper and folding to the bottom. Bring the ends together to create a half-fan. Secure with glue or staple. Glue the long, center edge of each half-fan together to make a circular fan.

★ Make two or three long tails from the fourth piece of paper.

★ Attach the center circle cut from the first piece of paper on top of the circular fan.

★ Attach the tails on the ribbon.

★ Add lettering for First Place or Champion on the face (center piece) of the ribbon. Then add name, event, date, horse's name, etc., onto ribbon tails.

Keep going!

★ Congratulations on becoming a First Place Junior Master Horseman!

Trail Talk: Share what the different colors of event ribbons mean (blue- 1st place, red- 2nd place, etc.). Talk about how winning awards can give a horseman a wonderful feeling, but participating and doing your best with your horse is the greatest reward of all.

Ride Further: Use these ideas to enjoy show ribbons in unique, fun ways:

★ Create more crazy colorful ribbons for awarding each other. Make up fun categories like the following: horseman with the best smile, fastest ride, oldest spurs, loudest laugh, best horse joke teller, etc. Or better yet, make show ribbons for your own horse to hang in the tack room so everyone can see how talented your animal is in many different ways.

★ Sew your show ribbons to a pillow or quilt, or make a collage picture to frame.

★ Set goals to award yourself and your horse when small and large goals are accomplished.

Chapter
7

Safety

Horse Behaviors ✕—✕—✕—✕—✕—✕—✕—✕—✕

As you learned in JMH Chapter One, horses are naturally sociable animals. This means they like to be around other animals they feel safe with. Although many horses are as gentle as the family pup, they *are* still animals, and they *can* be unpredictable. By becoming more aware of basic horsemanship skills, you will grow into a more responsible and safe-minded horseman.

Riding a horse is so much fun

PHOTO COURTESY OF AQHA

✕—✕—✕—✕—✕—✕—✕—✕—✕—✕—✕—✕—✕—✕

Barn Talk!

Let's get creative with words! If you were asked to come up with another name for a horse that doesn't spook easily (bombproof), what would it be? If you like playing with words, go back through your JMH handbook and have fun renaming other Horse Lingo words.

Basic Horsemanship: Mount Up!

… that is, when the tack is in place and the horse behaves! There are two important keys to remember before any ride begins: Each piece of tack should be checked and in place and the horse should be at ease. In the following activity, the steps to safely mount and dismount a horse will be explained and practiced.

Hold up! Before you put a leg up be sure to check for these things that might get you and your horse off to a poor start:

★ Twisted straps (reins, cinch, bridle, etc.)

★ Poor fitting blankets, saddle, bridle and bit

★ Loose or twisted cinch and girth

★ Stirrups (wrong type, size, or length)

★ Horseshoes aren't considered tack, but they are something extra attached to your horse's body, so take time to check them before riding

In the following activity, the routine of mounting (getting up into the saddle) and dismounting (getting out of the saddle and off your horse) will be practiced using some JMH imagination and a simple chair.

Keep going!

Objective: To learn basic skills needed to safely mount and dismount a horse

Time: 15 minutes

Materials: Simple chair without arms; Steps to Mounting Up!; Option: If you can, practice basic mounting and dismounting skills with a real horse AND another experienced horseman.

Saddle Up: Follow these steps to practice the correct way to mount a horse, which will actually be a chair in this activity.

PHOTOS COURTESY OF AQHA

Keep going!

Steps To Mounting Up!

First, face the chair (your horse) and give your ride a cue like a kind word or pat on the neck that you're about to mount up. Remember, you're mounting an imaginary horse so use your imagination to find the stirrups, saddle horn, or pommel.

1. After you've completed the safety check, stand on the left side of the horse even with the stirrup and facing the saddle.

2. Hold the reins in your left hand and rest the ball of the left foot (boot) in the stirrup on the stirrup bar (bottom part of stirrup).

3. Hold on to the saddle horn (Western saddle) or pommel (English saddle). Gently pull up and swing right leg over the saddle.

4. Place the right foot in the right stirrup.

5. Sit tall and even reins out on the horse's neck. Now that you are on top of the horse, take a look at the bridle and check how the saddle feels. If everything seems to be in the right place and cinched up tight, then you're ready to ride.

To dismount (get out of the saddle), reverse the steps above.

If you're a new horseman, soon these steps will become second nature, and you'll have it down in no time. It's also a good idea to know how to dismount off both sides, just in case you find yourself in a bind sometime and need to quickly get off from the right side.

Keep going!

Safety Tips for Mounting and Dismounting:

★ Don't get into a hurry to mount up if your horse is misbehaving. This might cause you to get hurt and doesn't help your horse develop good habits.

★ Ask for another horseman to hold your horse's head steady if you need some help with your horse while mounting or dismounting. It's okay to ask for help and the safest thing to do if your horse won't cooperate.

★ If your horse won't settle down, lead him to another area where he can calm down. Then mount or dismount. Remember, it's never a good idea to get on a horse that can't be controlled. Your safety and the safety of other horsemen should always come first.

Trail Talk: Talk about how horsemen can help each other mount up. The best way to do this is to clasp both hands together in a cup. Lower the hand so the rider can use the cup as a stirrup. Then count to three and give the rider a gentle lift.

Ride Further: Grow in your knowledge of riding skills by using these ideas:

★ Contact your local county extension agent, agricultural teacher, feed supply store, or local horse club to see if there are any horse camps that you could participate in to learn more about horses and horsemanship skills.

★ Practice! Practice! Practice! Spending time with your horse and in the company of another experienced horseman are the best ways to develop great horsemanship skills.

The Emergency or Unexpected Dismount

It's not enough for a man to know how to ride; he must know how to fall. ~ *Mexican Proverb*

Falling off your horse is not a good thing, unless you are a saddle bronc rider and your eight seconds is up! Horses will be horses, and they may buck when they feel frisky, spook, or get excited. Hopefully this never happens to you, but in case it does, it's wise to at least have thought about what you will do in this type of situation. In the following activity, you will be given three simple thoughts to memorize what to do and how to help someone else in this situation.

Objective: To memorize simple ideas to use in an emergency or unexpected dismount

Time: 10 minutes

Materials: Emergency or Unexpected Dismount reminders

Saddle Up: Here's some simple things to remember in an emergency or unexpected dismount:

1. **Feet Out**- Get your feet out of the stirrups as fast as you can!

Keep going!

2. **Let Go**- Do not hang on to the reins. This might get you and your horse tangled up … not good!

3. **Fall Away**- Fall or push away from the horse and get out of his way!

Make It Short And Simple By Saying, Feet Out, Let Go, Fall Away!

Now, say it using these motions:

1. **Feet Out** (Start with both feet together. Then hop out like you were doing a jumping jack.)

2. **Let Go** (Throw arms up!)

3. **Fall Away** (Fall or lunge back)

Repeat The Steps And Motions Until You Have It Down! For Fun, Say It Faster, Faster, And Faster! What a ride!

Now, to help someone else falling off, use these ideas:

★ Safety first. Call for help!

★ Help them remember what to do by calling out: **Feet Out, Let Go, Fall Away!**

★ If their horse is running, try to slow it down, close gates, or block it from leaving the area.

★ Don't do anything that might get you injured. You can't help another horseman in trouble if you are hurt, too.

Keep going!

Trail Talk: Share experiences where either you or another horseman had to make an emergency or unexpected dismount. What was the cause of the horse's excitement and what was the outcome?

Ride Further: There's a big arena of books and information out there waiting to be discovered. Use these ideas to explore the exciting world of rodeo and to learn more about being a safe rider and skilled horseman.

★ Check out the Professional Rodeo Cowboys Association site at ***www.prorodeo.org***. to learn more about how saddle bronc riders and bareback riders rig up and ride.

★ Visit (with supervision, of course!) the National Cowgirl Museum and Hall of Fame Web site at ***www.cowgirl.net.*** Here you can learn about the amazing women that helped pioneer America, and yes, even rode bucking broncs back in the early days of rodeo history.

PHOTO COURTESY OF AQHA

A Quick Lesson in Horse Talk

Horsemen know a language that few other humans know: horse talk. You can't learn this foreign language in a classroom, and it's not printed in any book. The best place to pick it up is around the barn, in the company of a horse, or by way of an experienced horseman. Horse talk is fun, easy, and a snap to learn, especially when you love horses. In the following activity, horse signals, messages, and responses will be explored by using horse knowledge and creative thinking skills

Objective: To become aware of ways horses communicate by using body and voice signals, and to use thinking and reasoning skills to fill in appropriate responses

Time: 30 minutes

Materials: Chart A and B below; pencil

Saddle Up: A horse communicates using his body and voice to send signals, like when he wants something or isn't sure about someone moving into his space. Read each area of the following chart. Then write down possible answers in the Horse Message and Horseman's Response areas. Think about what the horse is trying to communicate and what you could do to help the situation.

Keep going! ➡

Chart A

Read each horse signal and circle the correct horse message answer. Then write what you think a horseman (or you) could do to help the situation.

Horse Signal *(Body movements or behavior)*

The horse is sniffing at the water in the trough but won't take a drink.

Horse's Message *(What message is the horse trying to communicate?)*

A. This water is unclean!

B. Wonder where the goldfish went?

Horseman's Response *(What should the horseman do?)*

_____

_____

_____

_____

_____

Keep going!

Horse Signal *(Body movements or behavior)*

The horse trots away from the horseman as soon as he sees the halter.

Horse's Message *(What message is the horse trying to communicate?)*

A. I love to be caught.

B. Catch me if you can!

Horseman's Response *(What should the horseman do?)*

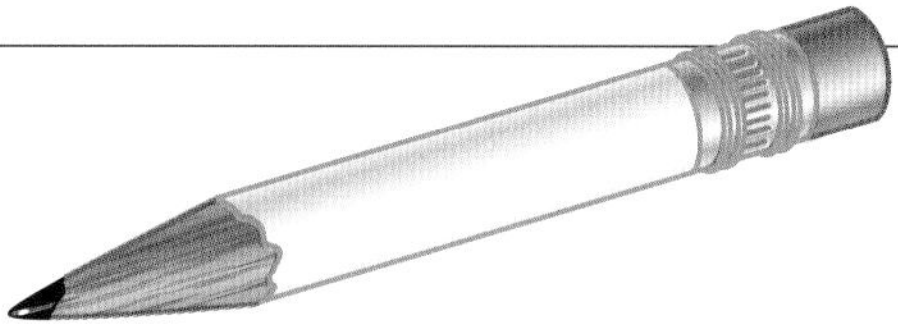

_____

_____

_____

_____

_____

_____

_____

_____

Keep going!

Horse Signal *(Body movements or behavior)*

The horse turns over the empty feed bucket and rolls it around the pen.

Horse's Message *(What message is the horse trying to communicate?)*

A. Can't anyone see that I'm ready to eat?

B. I don't like the color of my feed bucket.

Horseman's Response *(What should the horseman do?)*

_____

_____

_____

_____

_____

_____

_____

_____

Keep going!

Horse Signal *(Body movements or behavior)*

The horse swishes his tail and pins his ears when someone walks up from behind.

Horse's Message *(What message is the horse trying to communicate?)*

A. It's about time you got here.

B. Who are you and what do you want?

Horseman's Response *(What should the horseman do?)*

_____

_____

_____

_____

_____

_____

_____

_____

Keep going! →

Let's think more about how horses communicate with horsemen and other animals:

Horses are experts at: pawing, licking, kicking, swishing their tail, running, pitching, whinnying, throwing their head, chewing, biting, stamping their feet, pushing things around with their nose, and pinning or perking their ears.

Chart B

Read each horse message in the middle column. Think about what signals a horse might give for each message. Go back and fill in the horse signal area in the first column. Then circle the horseman's response in the last column that you think would be the best solution for the situation.

Horse's Message *(What message is the horse trying to communicate?)*

Who's there? Watch out! I don't like surprises.

Horseman's Response *(What should the horseman do?)*

A. Give the old horse a hard slap on the hindquarter.

B. Stop and begin talking calmly to the horse.

Horse Signal *(Body movements or behavior)*

_____

_____

_____

Horse's Message *(What message is the horse trying to communicate?)*

Look here! Someone forgot to lock the feed room door and I could use a little snack about now.

Horseman's Response *(What should the horseman do?)*

A. Make sure the horse can't get into feed storage.

B. Don't worry. The horse knows better than to eat before feeding time.

Horse Signal *(Body movements or behavior)*

_____

_____

_____

_____

_____

_____

_____

_____

Keep going!

Horse's Message *(What message is the horse trying to communicate?)*

Ouch, this bit is really rubbing some painful sores on the sides of my mouth.

Horseman's Response *(What should the horseman do?)*

A. Keep using this bit.

B. Check the bit size and bridle fit.

Horse Signal *(Body movements or behavior)*

_____

_____

_____

_____

_____

_____

_____

Keep going!

Horse's Message *(What message is the horse trying to communicate?)*

These horseflies are biting me from one end to the other!

Horseman's Response *(What should the horseman do?)*

A. Muck the stall, be sure the horse is dewormed and mist the horse with fly spray.

B. Keep a big horsefly swatter handy.

Horse Signal *(Body movements or behavior)*

_____

_____

_____

_____

_____

_____

_____

Keep going!

Trail Talk: Talk about how other animals, like dogs, cats, cattle, etc., use their bodies and voices to signal that they need something. Here's something else to ponder about how animals communicate: Anyone know how fish communicate that they are hungry or need clean water? Now, that's a tough one! But chances are that by the time the fish owner finds out, it's too late!

Ride Further: Learn more about communicating with a horse by using these ideas to grow in your horse communication skills:

★ Learn more about schooling and equine behavior by reading: *Western Horseman Magazine*

★ Observe or ride with trainers while they work or school horses as often as possible to learn proven methods and techniques

Rein in Language (Journal Writing)

Say it isn't so! You forgot it was show-and-tell day at school. Lucky for you, you have a picture in your notebook of you riding your horse. Quick! Write down the steps you go through to saddle up. Then when the teacher calls your name, you'll be ready to show the class the picture in your notebook and share the steps in saddling up your horse.

Habits of Good Horsemanship

Plan and prepare to become a champion Junior Master Horseman! In the following activity, habits of good horsemanship will be matched with reasons for practicing each habit of good horsemanship.

Objective: To use thinking and reasoning skills to match good habits of horsemanship and reasons for practicing each good habit

Time: 15 minutes

Materials: Chart on the next page; pencil

Saddle Up: No degree in rocket science needed here! Just match the Habits of Good Horsemanship in the left column with the reasons for practicing those habits in the right column.

PHOTO COURTESY OF ARABIAN HORSE ASSOCIATION

Keep going!

Good Horsemanship Matchup

**Habits of Good
Horsemanship**

**Reasons for Practicing
Habits of Good
Horsemanship**

A. Wear a safety helmet

_____ Keep your horse clean and checked for anything that might cause him to be uncomfortable or harmed during a ride.

B. Wear shoes/boots with a heel

_____ In case of emergency, it's always a good idea for someone else to know your whereabouts!

C. Wear fitted and protective clothing

_____ A loose girth, twisted straps, or poorly fitting bridle and bit can cause big problems!

D. Groom and check horse before saddling

_____ Clothes should be fitted enough to not catch on anything, protective, and comfortable to ride in.

E. Check tack

_____ Protecting your head might save you from making a trip to the hospital.

F. Let someone know where you are riding, when you will return home, and who you are with.

_____ Heeled shoes/boots keep the foot safely in the stirrup. Leather soles are best because they slide in and out of the stirrup easily.

Keep going!

See Appendix for answer key

Trail Talk: Talk about why it is important to wear protective clothing while riding and what kind of clothing is usually worn for riding in English and Western events.

Ride Further: Set a goal to learn more about how to be a safe-minded Junior Master Horseman by reading books about horses, horse behavior, and good horsemanship. Here are some books to get your library started:

★ The American Quarter Horse Foundation's Rising Star CD is made just for ambitious young horsemen like you! Go to ***www.quarterhorseoutfitters.com***

★ *The Horse Industry Handbook: A Guide to Equine Care and Management* (American Youth Horse Council)

DAVID STOECKLEIN PHOTO

PHOTO COURTESY OF AQHA

PHOTO COURTESY OF AQHA

Horse Lingo

★ When a horse is *barn sour*, he will not want to leave his stall. This behavior may be caused by a horse's poor attitude or bad experience. It can also be caused by the horse's dislike of doing the same thing over and over again.

★ *Manners under the saddle* are measured by how pleasant and willing the horse is while being ridden.

★ A *vice* is a bad behavior that a horse may develop because he is bored or copying another horse. Chewing, kicking, pacing, or running away are all bad vices that can be very hard to change.

★ A horse that is *bombproof* is one that doesn't spook easily.

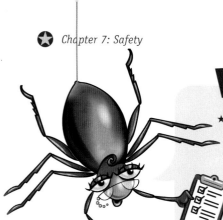

Did You Know?

★ Foals that are handled early in life usually respond to training better.

★ Horses learn from each other. Training a young horse around other well-behaved horses can help teach good ground manners and overall good behavior.

★ Don't let your guard down! Even a gentle horse may scare at a sudden loud noise or quick movement.

★ The official name for rodeo bronc busting is bareback riding or saddle bronc riding.

Behavior Around Horses

Understanding the horse and basic horsemanship can help make owning, showing, and riding a horse one of the most rewarding experiences in the world. Spending time around horses and other seasoned horsemen are the best ways to give yourself that strong leg up to become the best Junior Master Horseman you can be!

PHOTO COURTESY OF ApHC

Barn Talk!

You're an Inventor!

You have just invented a horse-friendly device that is selling like hotcakes! This device translates what a horse is thinking into messages a horseman can understand. Draw a picture of this high-tech device. Share how it works, how much it costs, and where it can be purchased ... and don't forget to give your device a catchy brand name.

JMH Pledge

What is a pledge? A pledge is a personal promise to support a special cause or purpose. How about taking a pledge to become the best horseman you can be? In the following activity, the Junior Master Horseman pledge will be practiced using a little bit of memory and a whole lot of heart.

Objective: To use memory and language skills to practice and recite the Junior Master Horseman pledge

Time: Unlimited

Materials: Junior Master Horseman Pledge; practice fill-in-the-blank exercise; pencil

Saddle Up: The brain is an amazing machine, and if you haven't heard, not everyone learns in the same way … thank goodness! One person's brain may record and store what it sees and hears in a different way than someone else's. Just take a look at some of the different ways that information can be learned. Then use whichever one works best for you in the following activity, and remember … you can do it!

★ Mimic: Listen to someone read the print one sentence at a time. Practice repeating each sentence with the speaker until you know the passage by heart. You can do it!

Keep going!

★ Word association: Look at each sentence and find key words to underline or highlight. For example, in the first sentence, focus on the word **treat**, then place the words **safe** and **respectful** in your mind as connecting with the word **treat**. It works. Before long, the word **treat** will trigger your mind to also think of **safe** and **respectful**. You can do it!

★ Write: One great way to remember a thought or idea is to practice copying it over and over. Before long, you will be able to write the passage without even looking at the copy. You can do it!

★ Fill-in-the-blanks: Copy the passage. Then erase key words. Practice reading and saying the passage. Then go back and fill in the blank spaces by memory. You can do it!

Take it away, Junior Master Horseman...

Junior Master Horseman Pledge

I _____ will treat myself, my horse, and other horsemen in a safe and respectful way. But above all, I will be a dependable, responsible horseman and a positive example for other horsemen to follow.

Don't pass up this next go-round. Practice your fill-in-the-blank skills right here and now. Then after you finish, look at the pledge above to check your answers. Remember, you can do it, practice does make perfect, and the harder you work, the better you'll get!

Junior Master Horseman Pledge

I _____ will treat myself, my

_____, and other horsemen in a _____ and

_____ way. But above all, I will be a _____,

_____ horseman and a _____ example

for other _____ to follow.

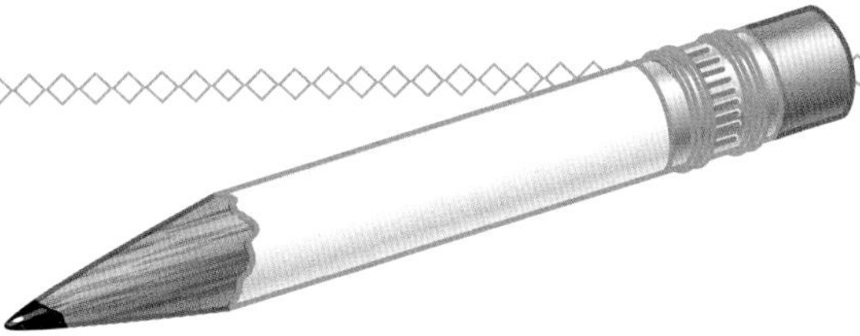

Keep going!

Trail Talk: Talk about other pledges that are familiar like the Pledge of Allegiance, 4-H or FFA pledges, and the pledges recited by the Girl Scouts and Boy Scouts.

Ride Further:

★ Make up another original pledge using ideas from the Junior Master Horseman Pledge.

★ Design an original flag to go with the Junior Master Horseman Pledge.

★ The Star Spangled Banner started out as a poem. Then it was later put to music and became the National Anthem. Think of a familiar, simple song or rhythm that the Junior Master Horseman Pledge could be adapted to.

Horse Lingo

★ A horse's *ground manners* can be measured by the way he acts during grooming and saddling. A good-mannered horse is a safe horse!

★ A *quick-release knot* is the safest way to tether, or tie, a horse.

★ The fold of a knot is called the *bight*.

Ready, set ... Quick-Release Knot!

So what's all the talk about tying a horse lead with a quick-release knot? Think **quick** and **release**. This way of tying a lead rope is a must for keeping the horse and everyone around the horse as safe as possible, especially during an emergency. Always use the quick-release knot for tying a horse to a strong post, and always keep a watchful eye on a tied horse. In the following activity, tying and untying the quick-release knot will be practiced and timed.

But first, take a look at these tips that could help keep a horse and horseman safe while tying:

★ Tie horse with a length of around two feet (about an arm's length) of lead rope.

★ Be sure to use a quick-release knot.

★ Tie away from strange or unsettled horses, or close to feed and water that might cause the horse to be anxious or break away.

Objective: To learn how to safely tie and untie a horse lead using a quick-release knot

Time: 30 minutes

Keep going!

Materials: Steps to Tying the Quick-Release Knot; lead rope, heavy string, or small rope (pigging string), etc., for tying practice. A shoestring, single rein, or a man's suit tie can even be used!

Saddle Up: knot kidding … A knot is safe and useful when it is easy to tie, untie, and stays secure under pressure.

With rope in hand, follow the steps below to practice tying a quick-release knot. When you're ready, time yourself or create some friendly knot tying competition with another horseman.

How to Tie a Quick-Release Knot

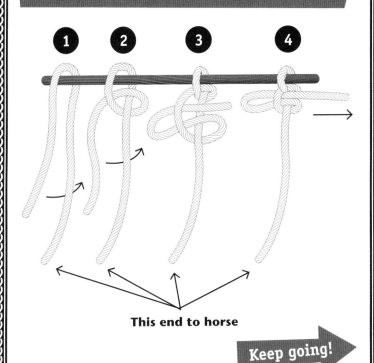

This end to horse

Keep going!

Kick up your knot-tying skills another notch or two by wearing a blindfold or turning the lights off while tying the quick-release knot. When you become a success without using your sight, then you've got the knack of tying the quick-release knot!

Trail Talk: Share ideas about how to tie and protect a horse in areas where there is traffic or curious people that might spook or bother a horse tied without supervision. Just a reminder: It's never a safe or good idea to leave a tied horse unattended.

Ride Further: Take a look these interesting knot names and words associated with knot tying:

Common Knot Names:

Thumb Knot; Figure-Eight Knot; Sheetbend; Square Knot; Clove Hitch; Rolling Hitch; Bloodknot; Clinch Knot

Knot Vocabuary:

Knot: A knot stops a line from continuing in a line or rope.

Stopper knots: Knots used to keep the end of a rope from fraying, or to keep a line from entering a small space.

Bend: A bend is used to join two ropes together.

Hitch: A hitch is used to tie a rope to a ring or post.

Running End: The end of the rope used to tie the knot.

Standing End: The open end of the rope.

Bight: This can be the part of the rope in between the two ends, or where the rope bends to form a loop.

Jam: This happens when the knot tightens under tension and becomes difficult or impossible to untie.

How to Safely Pick Up a Horse's Foot

Did you know that horse hooves can grow from 1/2 to 3/8 of an inch per month? This means that someone is going to need to check, clean, trim, and shoe them from time to time, usually every six to eight weeks. Some horses are finicky (fussy) about having their feet picked up.

Knowing these basics about how to safely pick up a horse's foot is an important skill for every horseman to learn and practice.

★ First, always have an experienced horseman close by.

★ Be sure the horse is tied to a strong post.

★ Tools for cleaning hooves should be handy once you have the horse's foot in your hand.

In the following activity, the correct way to pick up a horse's foot will be practiced in a safe way.

Objective: To better understand and practice how to safely pick up a horse's foot

Time: 20 minutes

Keep going!

Materials: Horseman; Option: If you have a real horse or access to a real horse, then grab an experienced horseman and practice this important skill.

Saddle Up: For a safe pick-up, follow these steps by first practicing on a horseman. Then if you have access to a real horse and experienced horseman, use your new skills to practice safely picking up and letting down horse feet.

To practice safely picking up a horse's front foot, have a two-legged friend get down on all fours (hands and knees). For practicing safely picking up the back feet, have the horseman stand. Be ready for your friend to move around, stomp, or kick like a real horse would…just for fun, of course!

PHOTO COURTESY OF AMERICAN QUARTER HORSE JOURNAL

1. Make sure the horse is haltered and tied to a strong post and tied with a quick-release knot (Explained in the previous JMH activity)

2. Stand beside the horse's shoulder, facing toward the rear end of the horse.

Keep going!

3. To pick up the horse's left front foot or left back foot, run your inside hand from the forearm area down the leg to the fetlock (ankle) to grasp the tuft of fetlock hair. Gently lift foot.

4. If the horse doesn't cooperate easily, gently put pressure under the fetlock to encourage the horse to lift the foot. You can also lean on the leg gently to push the horse's weight onto his other side.

5. Hold the lifted foot with left hand.

6. Check and clean hoof parts and horseshoe with, right hand.

7. Ease the foot down.

To continue on the right side, repeat steps and use the right (inside) hand to hold each foot while checking or cleaning.

Trail Talk: Talk about what a horseman should do if a horse won't allow anyone to touch his feet. Share ideas about why a young horseman should NOT check an unpredictable or injured horse's foot (or feet).

Ride Further: Do your best to learn more about handling horse feet in a safe way by using these ideas:

★   Observe a local farrier's skills in handling horse feet.

★   Improve skills at picking up and letting down animal feet by practicing on a smaller, tame animal like a dog, friendly sheep or goat, or a gentle miniature horse.

★   Make time as often as you can to groom and handle your horse.

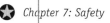

Did You Know?

★ To ride with good balance, sit deep in the saddle with a straight back.

★ The key to riding safely and staying in the saddle is to feel the horse's movement and move along with him or her in unison (at the same time).

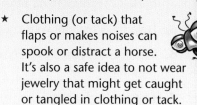

★ Clothing (or tack) that flaps or makes noises can spook or distract a horse. It's also a safe idea to not wear jewelry that might get caught or tangled in clothing or tack.

★ A novice (new or inexperienced) rider should not practice mounting without the supervision of a seasoned (or experienced) horseman. Remember, safety first!

Howdy Horsemen!

Don't forget to wrangle your parents up to the computer and register at **www.JuniorMasterHorseman.com!**

JMH Door Knob Hanger

Better be safe than sorry, as the old saying goes. It's always a good idea to let others know where you are and what you are doing, just in case there is an emergency or you are needed for some important reason. This is especially true for horsemen riding or working around large animals. In the following activity, a JMH Door Knob Hanger will be cut out, filled in, and used as a safety measure for keeping everyone in-the-know about what's going on in and around the barn.

Objective: To become more aware of how to be a more responsible horseman and to create a special door knob hanger

Time: 15 minutes

Materials: JMH Door Knob Hanger; pencil; Option: Laminate hanger and use dry erase markers

Saddle Up: Cut out the JMH Door Knob Hanger, fill it in and leave it on your bedroom door knob whenever you scoot out to spend time with your horse or friends. Option: Laminate the door knob sign and keep dry erase markers handy to write with so the sign can be used over and over again.

Keep going!

JMH Horseman

Sorry, I'm not available right now because I am busy...
(Check a circle below)

○ Riding   ○ In The Tack Room

○ Feeding   ○ Exercising My Horse

○ Grooming

○ Mucking Out   ○ Other:
The Stalls

_____

_____

Please leave me a message here:

_____

_____

_____

Thank you and Happy Trails!

TRIM HERE

TRIM HERE

JMH Horseman

_____

Sorry, I'm not available right now because I am busy...
(Check a circle below)

◯ Doing Homework

◯ Cleaning my Room

◯ In the Kitchen

◯ On the Computer

◯ Helping Someone

◯ Other:

_____

_____

Please leave me a message here:

_____

_____

_____

Thank you and Happy Trails!

TRIM HERE ✂

TRIM HERE ✂

Trail Talk: Talk about why it is always a good idea that others know where you are when you are riding alone or working around animals.

Ride Further: If you don't have a horse close by to care for or ride, or if you want to make another door knob hanger to use for other reasons, then fill in this blank hanger to suit yourself!

Rein in Language (Journal Writing)

Ever tried to outsmart a horse that doesn't want to be haltered? A large publisher has just contacted you to share your horse-catching secrets. Write down what works best for you (or what you think might work best) when it comes to catching a horse that has become very good at avoiding the halter.

Life Skills
& Careers

Chapter 8: Life Skills and Careers

Life Skills ✕—✕—✕—✕—✕—✕—✕—✕—✕—✕—✕

Spending time around a horse can teach a horseman many worthwhile life skills like responsibility, work ethic, friendship, patience, and tolerance for others (animals and humans), just to name a few. Animals, especially horses, are some of Mother Nature's best teachers, and everyone can learn a lot from spending more time around them … that's for sure!

DAVID STOECKLEIN PHOTO

PHOTO COURTESY OF AQHA

Barn Talk!

What Cue Would You do?

If you could pick only one horse-riding cue to use on a green broke horse (a horse that is newly trained and still unpredictable), what cue would it be and why would you choose this *one* cue over all of the others?

JMH Traders Day

Trading used tack, riding clothes, grooming tools, supplies, and equipment in good condition is a great way to keep a horseman and tack room in tip-top shape. In the following activity, some mighty good (and supervised) horse trading will commence (happen) in a fun and useful way.

Objective: To become aware that there are other creative ways to replace usable tack, riding clothes, grooming tools, supplies, and equipment

Time: Unlimited

Materials: Donated or available tack, riding clothes, grooming tools, supplies, and equipment

Saddle Up: Set a date to do some serious horse trading with other horsemen by using these ideas:

★ Gather up (with permission, please!) any horse-related items in good shape or working order that could be used for tack, riding attire (clothing), grooming, or barn supplies.

★ Invite local feed and tack stores to donate items they no longer carry or need, including feed or products that could be raffled or used for door prizes.

Keep going!

★ Prepare posters, place an ad in the newspaper, check horse web sites for sales, and contact local horse clubs to let everyone know about the Junior Master Horseman Horse Traders Day. Invite local horsemen to bring an item to add to what you have already rounded up.

★ For horse traders that want to raise money for a worthy cause, make and sell homemade JMH horse treats (Chapter Five Activity: Horse Cuisine: Horse Healthy Treats and horseman snacks).

Trail Talk: Talk about how the concept of recycling and conservation can be used in the horse business. Talk about how sharing rides to the vet or events could help cut travel expenses and conserve energy.

Ride Further: Become more aware of how horsemen trade horses, tack, supplies, and equipment by checking these resources:

★ newspaper classifieds

★ feed store bulletin boards

★ horse association magazines and Internet sites (with supervision)

★ local horse club information

★ show or event officials

Hey, what about starting your own horse trading newsletter or setting up shop at an event by inviting other horsemen to bring their own goods to trade and swap at shows? It's an enterprising thought!

Move 'Em Up, Head 'Em Out!

Before you head out on a cattle drive, trail ride, or trot across the pasture, make sure you know some basics about how to communicate with a horse. If you've ever been snow skiing, you understand that knowing how to safely stop is much more important than knowing how to race down the mountain! Same goes for riding a horse. Galloping may look really fun, but it's knowing how to guide the horse to a safe stop that makes all the difference!

First, let's take a look at two words that will help you better understand how a horseman communicates with a horse and why a well-trained horse behaves like a well-trained horse should:

Cue: A cue is some type of signal or stimuli that communicates what you want the horse to do. For example, when you squeeze both legs and give a gentle kick with your heels, a well-trained horse's response will be to move out with ease and not spook, buck, or run.

Response: A response is the action or result of the cue. For example, if you gently pull back on the reins, a well-trained horse's response will be to slow down or halt, depending on the bit pressure.

Keep going!

In the following activity, basic riding cues and horse responses will be practiced through role-play (acting out).

Objective: To demonstrate awareness of basic riding cues (commands) and horse responses that a horseman would expect from a well-trained horse

Time: 15 minutes

Materials: Cue and response list below

Saddle Up: No one has to teach a horse how to eat; that's a natural response. But a horse does have to be taught to be tame around humans and trained to understand riding cues. Take a look at the following basic cues. Imagine yourself horseback. Then demonstrate (show) each cue and the response you would expect your well-trained horse to make after each cue:

Riding Cue	Horse's Response
Whoa (verbal)	Horse will stop or stand still
Heel kick or verbal cue to go	Horse will move out with ease
Lower leg and heel pressure from the left	Horse will move right
Lower leg and heel pressure from the right	Horse will move left
Reins left	Horse will turn left
Reins right	Horse will turn right
Reins pulled back	Horse will slow or halt, depending on bit pressure

Now, find a friend and have them call out each riding cue so you can show them your skills at communicating with a horse. Then you'll know that you're ready to head 'em up and move 'em out!

Trail Talk: Are there other ways that horses can be given cues? Share ideas about using whips and spurs. Discuss how each artificial aid can be used in a sensitive and correct way.

Ride Further: Play games with riding cues by using these fun ideas:

★ Play a game of Simon Says using riding cues and horse responses.

★ Gather up a group of horsemen on imaginary horses in an imaginary horse arena. Call out each cue for horsemen to respond. Speed up calling out each cue. If a horseman doesn't respond correctly, he or she is out. Play until only one horseman is left. That person will be the cue caller for the next round.

★ Reverse things now! Role-play each horse response from the list. Ask horsemen to guess which cue goes with each response.

PHOTO COURTESY OF ARABIAN HORSE ASSOCIATION

DON STINE PHOTO

JMH Horse Drivers License

Driving any kind of moving object is a big responsibility! To drive a vehicle, a person must first know how to make the vehicle move forward, backward, slow down, speed up, turn, and of course, stop! These are many of the same movements that a horseman will have to know to safely and successfully ride a horse.

To get an official drivers license, most states require the driver to be a certain age and pass a driving test. In the following activity, a JMH Horse Drivers License will be earned by demonstrating basic riding cues and horse responses.

Objective: To demonstrate understanding of basic riding cues and horse responses

Time: 15 minutes

Materials: JMH Horse Drivers License Test and JMH Drivers License form

Saddle Up: Each horseman wanting to earn a JMH Horse Drivers License will need a tester (person to give the drivers license test). Follow the directions:

Keep going!

Tester: The goal is for the horseman to show you his/her understanding of basic riding cues by acting out the responses to each cue you call out. After every cue/response line has been checked, then fill out the JMH Horse Drivers License form and present it to the Junior Master Horseman with a strong hand shake and big congrats!

JMH Horse Drivers License Test

Tester: Say each cue, then check the box after correct response
Horseman: Respond to each cue

Tester's Cues	Horseman's Responses
❏ Whoa (verbal)	Horse will stop or stand still
❏ Heel kick or verbal cue to go	Horse will move out with ease
❏ Lower leg and heel pressure from the left	Horse will move right
❏ Lower leg and heel pressure from the right	Horse will move left
❏ Reins left	Horse will turn left
❏ Reins right	Horse will turn right
❏ Reins pulled back	Horse will slow or halt, depending on bit pressure

Keep going!

JMH Horse Drivers License Form

Junior Master Horseman Department of Life Skills

~ *Official* ~

HORSE DRIVERS LICENSE

Junior Master Horseman,

_____,

has successfully demonstrated knowledge of
basic horse riding cues and horse responses.

Congratulations!

Tester Signature _____

Junior Master Horseman Signature

_____

Date _____

Trail Talk: Share other cues that horses understand like the honking of a horn, the rattling of a feed bucket, or the shaking of a feed sack at feeding time. Then name other jobs or occupations that a license is needed for, like practicing veterinary medicine, hauling a commercial trailer load of rodeo stock, or working as a paramedic at a horse event.

Ride Further: Make copies of the form on the previous page. Then help other horsemen earn their own JMH Horse Drivers License!

Horse Lingo

★ *Whoa* in horse lingo simply means: *STOP!*

★ *Hold hard* is a hunting command that means to stop immediately!

★ To cowboys on the trail, the word *chuck* meant food! However, the word *chuck* is from an old English term meaning the cheapest cut of meat on a carcass. Interesting!

★ The name, *Cookie,* is what most chuck wagon cooks have been called ever since the chuck wagon was invented in 1866.

★ *Artificial aids* used by horsemen are man-made pieces of tack or equipment like spurs and whips.

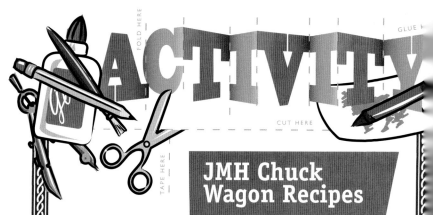

JMH Chuck Wagon Recipes

Did you know that understanding how to follow a recipe, measuring ingredients, and cooking are all important life skills? If you could whip up your favorite grub in the kitchen or out on the trail, what would it be?

_____ Sounds delicious!

Now, read the riddle below and try your best to not look at the answer until you've given the riddle some good thought!

Riddle: What do you call a Western-style portable kitchen on wheels?

Here's the low-down on the **chuck wagon**: The first chuck wagon (or at least one of the first recorded) was invented back in 1866 by former Texas Ranger and rancher Charles Goodnight. Goodnight owned the first cattle ranch in the Texas Panhandle, called the JA Ranch, located in Palo Duro Canyon. Goodnight also helped create the Goodnight-Loving Trail, which was a major cattle drive route from Texas through eastern New Mexico and Colorado.

These rolling kitchens, usually pulled by mules, oxen, or horses, carried basic vegetables (beans, corn, peas, cabbage). Meats like beef, bison, and sometimes a lucky catch of fish would be served up hot out of the iron skillet. Breads like quick-biscuits, sourdough bread, and

Keep going!

Answer: Chuckwagon

skillet cornbread gave cowhands another way to slop up the last bite on their plate. And no meal would be complete without a good hot cup of strong cowboy coffee … the kind you can stand a spoon up in!

Chuck wagons not only carried food, water, pots, pans, and eating utensils for the trail boss and cowhands, they also stored supplies, tools, and bedrolls. Chuck wagons are still used today on the ranch and trail rides, and competitive events like chuck wagon racing and cook-offs have never been more popular. In the following activity, some fun JMH Chuck Wagon recipes will be shared to lasso in some delicious food for hungry Junior Master Horsemen and friends.

Objective: To become more aware of the historic role of the chuck wagon along America's cattle trails and to follow a recipe to prepare JMH Chuck Wagon recipes

Time: Unlimited

Materials: JMH Chuck Wagon recipes (Ingredients and directions below)

Saddle Up: Have fun making and sharing these trail-bust'n JMH Chuck wagon recipes!

Keep going!

Chuck Wagon Recipes!

JMH Chuck Wagon Beans-N-Cheese

Ingredients
1 pack of franks (hot dogs)
1 can of Ranch Style Beans or pork n' beans
6 slices of sandwich cheese or cubed Velveeta
1 iron skillet lightly rubbed with a little cooking oil, shortening, or pat of butter

Directions
Cut up franks into bite size pieces. Mix with beans and cheese. Stir over medium heat until warm. **That's it! Dig in!**

JMH Chuck Wagon Pizza Roll

Ingredients
Pre-made pizza crust
Favorite pizza sauce, cheese(s), and toppings
Aluminum foil

Directions
Lay crust on foil. Add sauce, cheese(s), and toppings. Roll crust up like you would a burrito. Cover with foil and cook over medium heat until hot. **Come and get it!**

JMH Chuck Wagon Garlic Biscuits And Buttery Cinnamon Buttons

For Garlic Biscuits:

Ingredients
1 can of buttermilk biscuits
2 T. melted butter with
1 T. garlic

Directions
Lightly spray pan, skillet, or cookie sheet with non-stick spray, oil, or butter. Place biscuits close touching sides. Brush biscuit tops with melted garlic butter. Cook in an oven at 400 degrees for 12-15 minutes or over campfire until fluffy and hot. Biscuits may also be wrapped in foil for cooking. (Cover with lid or foil when cooking over open fire.)

For Buttery Cinnamon Buttons:

Ingredients
1 can of buttermilk biscuits
2 T. melted butter
sugar cinnamon mixture

Directions
Form biscuits into small balls. Roll each ball in melted butter. Sprinkle with sugar cinnamon mixture. Place biscuits (touching) in pan, cast-iron skillet, or on cookie sheet and cook at 400 degrees for 15 minutes or until fluffy and golden brown on top. Biscuits may also be wrapped in foil for cooking. Whew-doggie! Dee-licious!

Trail Talk: Share other fun, simple recipes from home (or make some up) that would be delicious on a chuck wagon menu. Name supplies that you think would be the most important for a chuck wagon boss to have in his moving kitchen.

Ride Further: Use these ideas to further explore cooking along America's cattle trails:

★ Add Pioneer recipes to your collection by expoloring books in your local library and book stores.

★ Collect recipes that you think would make great chuckwagon grub by interviewing family members and friends.

PHOTO COURTESY OF AMERICAN QUARTER HORSE JOURNAL

Did You Know?

★ Most horses today are used for leisure purposes. Horse holidays and horse vacations are becoming more and more popular for horsemen that like to enjoy their horse in relaxing and adventurous ways.

★ If you repeatedly kick or flap your legs on the horse's sides, this may eventually teach the horse to ignore your cue to move out at all!

★ In a good square halt, the horse stops standing on all fours and the rider is balanced in the saddle.

★ Besides feeding the trail boss and all of the cowhands, the chuck wagon cook was also everyone's barber, banker, and many times, a referee whenever the cowhands had arguments and fights.

Rein in Language (Journal Writing)

What you think counts! Write down basic things you think every horseman should know in order to ride a horse. Compare your list with other horsemen. Talk about how each list is different and reflects your experience and interest in horses.

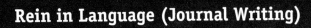

Careers

Some people grow up knowing they want to work around horses, and others just luck out and find themselves working in the horse industry anyway! It's a great and growing field, so if you never want to be too far away from what's happening in the world of horses, then saddle up and set your sights on a career studying, training, breeding, riding, or working in one of the many fields the horse industry has to offer.

By the way ... if you could work around horses when you grow up, what would you most like to do?

Jockey? Cowboy? Cowgirl? Trainer? Vet?

DVM Interview

When you think about what you want to be when you grow up, what comes to mind? If you love animals, you might want to consider becoming a DVM (Doctor of Veterinary Medicine). Some veterinarians specialize in caring for small animals, like dogs and cats. Other veterinarians focus on treating large animals, like cattle and horses. And don't forget all the many small and large wild animals living in zoos and wildlife reserves around the world … they need a doctor's care, too! In the following activity, the task at hand will be to interview a DVM, then share personal thoughts and ideas about this animal-riffic profession!

Objective: To experience an interview and share perspectives through written language

Time: Two Interviews (approx. 30 minutes each)

Materials: Interview form; camera

Saddle Up: Contact your favorite veterinary clinic. Introduce yourself and ask to schedule a short (30 minute) interview with the large animal veterinarian. Make a courtesy call on the interview day to remind the vet that you are coming. Dress neatly. Bring along a camera to take pictures (Be sure to ask permission before snapping pictures of animals and people visiting the clinic).

Keep going!

Place your interview form on a clipboard and have your pencil ready to write. Fill in the top part of the interview form before you arrive at the clinic. This will show the person you are interviewing that you are prepared and respect his/her time away from taking care of the animals in the waiting room!

Doctor of Veterinary Medicine

Interview

Date _____ **Time of Interview** _____

My Name _____

Age _____

Name of Veterinarian _____

_____

Phone _____

Clinic Address _____

Circle type of animal practice:

Large   Small   Both Large and Small

Begin by saying:

Junior Master Horseman: Hello. My name is Junior Master Horseman (your name) _____. Before we begin, I would like to thank you for allowing me to interview you about being a veterinarian. Are you ready to begin?

Then Ask:

Interview Questions

1. What schools did you attend and how many years did it take you to earn your degree as a veterinarian?

_____

2. When did you know you wanted to be an equine (large animal) veterinarian?

_____

3. How many years have you been a veterinarian?

_____

4. On average, how many horses do you treat each day?

_____

5. What is the most challenging and most rewarding part of your job?

_____

6. Have any of your patients (horses or other animals) ever hurt you?

_____

7. What diseases or conditions do you treat horses for the most?

_____

8. If you were not a vet, what would you be?

_____

9. If you could name one word that explains your profession, what would it be?

_____

End the interview by saying:

Junior Master Horseman: Thank you for allowing me to interview you. You have been very helpful! Before I go, are there any questions that you would like to ask me?

On a separate piece of paper, write your thoughts and ideas about what it would be like to be a Doctor of Veterinary Medicine.

Trail Talk: If you could ask the veterinarian one more interview question, what would it be? Share what it was like to talk one-on-one with a real working DVM.

Ride Further: Did you know that some dentists work on wild animals, like elephants, tigers, and alligators? Ask your local vet if he has ever treated undomesticated (wild) animals in his clinic or at the local zoo.

Barn Talk!

What's Your Dream Job?

Come up with a new career and career name for the horse industry. Think about creating an interesting career that might be added to words like specialist, master, trainer, or manager. How about being a saddle master or jockey specialist? Sounds interesting!

Western Artist: Your Career Begins Here!

Ever thought about being a Western artist? Many horsemen collect art and are artists themselves. One of America's most famous Western artists was Frederic Remington (1861-1909). His sketches, paintings, and bronzes are some of the most valuable and sought after masterpieces of Western art ever created. In the following activity, homemade playdough will be made and used to create an original piece of art sculpture.

Objective: To become more aware of Western art and to encourage artistic expression through art

Time: 45 minutes

Materials: Playdough ingredients, supplies, and sculpting tools (spoon, fork, pop cycle stick, bendable wire, small wooden twigs from outside, horse pictures and horse figures).

Optional: Other sculpting supplies that professional sculptors might also use are:

★ Roma Plastilina (brand name) sculpting clay never hardens so it can be worked and reworked over and over and is the clay used by most professional sculptors

Keep going!

★ Lazy Susan- Find an old Lazy Susan (turntable) to keep clay on while sculpting. Being able to turn your sculpture around while working on it will give you an easy glance at every angle.

★ Professional sculpting tools can be found at most hobby stores. However, keep in mind that many things at home can be used for sculpting.

Saddle Up: Make the JMH Artist Playdough recipe. Please be aware that this dough recipe will harden as it drys. Begin sculpting by forming simple objects like an apple, horseshoe, or riding boot. Then move on to shaping a horse's head. To make a horse's body, first make a stick form with bendable wire or wooden twigs glued or wired together from outside. Use a picture of a horse to look at while you sculpt. It just takes some time, practice, and patience. Set a goal to create a new piece every week. Who knows? You may be the next great Western artist. And just think … it all started in your quest to become a Junior Master Horseman. Follow the directions to make your playdough and get started!

JMH Artist Playdough

Ingredients

3 cups flour,
1/4 cup salt,
1 cup water,
1T vegetable oil
extra flour and water for adjusting mixture.
Option: Acrylic paints

Directions

Mix 3 cups of flour with 1/4 cup of salt. Add 1 cup of water with your choice of food coloring and 1T vegetable oil. If the mixture is too stiff, add a few drops of water. If the mixture is too sticky, add more flour. Keep dough stored in a cool place in plastic bags or in a covered container. Dough works best at room temperature.

Mold playdough into shapes. Dough will dry if left out, so if you want to start over, just roll dough in a ball and place it back in a plastic bag or container. Dough can also be painted when dry.

Keep going!

Trail Talk: Share ideas about your favorite kind of art. Keep in mind that many artists enjoy more than one medium (style or technique) of art, just like Frederic Remington, an accomplished illustrator AND sculptor.

Ride Further: Explore more about sculpture and famous sculptors by using these ideas:

★ Explore local museums that showcase western art.

★ Visit (with supervision) the following museum Web site for more fascinating information about American artist Frederic Remington: ***www.fredericremington.org***.

★ You can't learn about sculpture without knowing more about the famous Michelangelo (1475-1564). He carved the famous marble statue of David (modeled after the biblical hero, David) that stands over 14 feet tall at the Galleria dell'Accademia, Florence, Italy. Another one of his most treasured works that can still be seen today is the ceiling of the Sistine Chapel (Vatacan) in Rome.

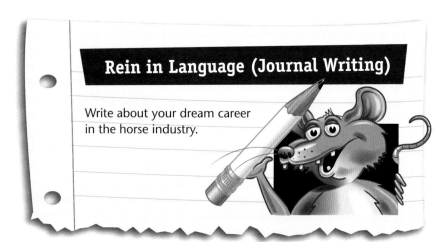

Rein in Language (Journal Writing)

Write about your dream career in the horse industry.

Horse Industry Career Word Scramble

Have you ever wondered what you might like to do when you grow up? If you're interested in working in the horse industry, there are more careers for horse lovers than you can shake a stick at! How about being a trainer, veterinarian, or a dude ranch manager? The horse industry needs scientists, sales representatives, accountants, ranchers, search and rescue teams, breeders, and folks to engineer safer horse trailers … and that's just the tip of the haystack! In the following activity, horse industry career words will be unscrambled using hints (beside each scrambled word) and a word box (below).

Objective: To use word association and creative thinking skills to unscramble horse industry career words

Time: 20 minutes

Materials: JMH Word Scramble and Horse Industry Career Word Box (on the following pages)

Keep going!

Saddle Up: Use the hints and word box below to write each horse industry career word correctly:

JMH Word Scramble

nnetvireaari *(animal doctor)*

v _ _ _ _ i _ _ r _ _ n

tistar *(creative with art)*

a _ _ _ s _

jltouranis *(writer)*

_ o _ _ n _ l _ _ t

eebrder *(breeds horses)*

b _ e _ _ _ r

erost geraman *(2 words- manages a store)*

s _ _ r _   m _ n _ _ e _

anerchr *(runs or owns a ranch)*

r _ n _ _ _ r

aless evitatsenerpre *(2 words- seller of goods and services)*

s _ l _ s   r _ p _ _ s _ _ t a _ _ v _

JMH Word Scramble *(cont.)*

eraintr *(teacher of horses)*

__ r __ __ n __ r

eyockj *(race horse rider)*

j __ __ k __ __

orseh tliscispea *(2 words- horse expert)*

h __ __ __ e   __ p __ c __ __ __ i __ t

rierrfa *(trims and shoes horses)*

__ a r __ i __ __

hows geraman *(2 words- manages event or show)*

s __ o __   m __ n __ g __ __

istentsci *(research expert)*

s __ i __ n __ __ s __

Horse Industry Career Word Box

show manager   farrier   horse specialist   jockey

trainer   sales representative   rancher   store manager

breeder   journalist   artist   veterinarian   scientist

Trail Talk: Talk about other careers in the horse industry not listed in the word box. Talk about what kind of experience or education is needed to work in each career field.

Ride Further: Choose your favorite horse career, then find out more about it by reading books and talking to others who have similar interests or careers in the horse industry.

Horse Lingo

★ To *teach or train a horse* is called schooling.

★ A *horse specialist* is someone who is an expert on horses.

★ A *groom* is someone that grooms horses.

★ An *equine geneticist* is a scientist that would know everything scientific about the horse species, including horse DNA.

Did You Know?

★ The equine world is a Multi-billion industry.

★ Millions of people work in the horse industry.

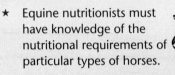

★ A pedigree analyst is an expert at researching horse lineage (family background) and registration information.

★ Equine nutritionists must have knowledge of the nutritional requirements of particular types of horses.

★ An equine insurance agent sells insurance policies to horse owners. These policies can help protect a horseman's financial investment in horses, buildings, tack, trailers, trucks, and equipment.

★ Riding horses helps develop important self-esteem and social skills. Now, that's important!

Happy Trails Horseman!

Go to JuniorMasterHorseman.com to complete your comprehension check and print your certificate. See you down the trail in Level 2!

Appendix A

{ Answer Keys for Chapters 2-7 }

Chapter 2, page 45

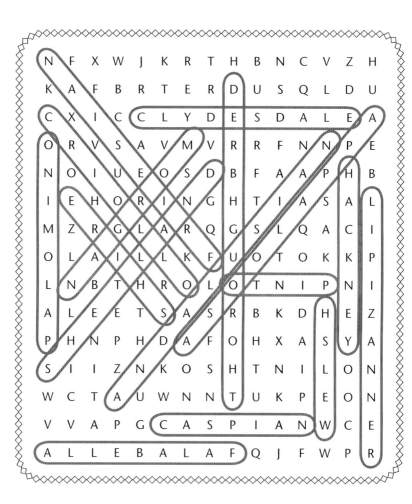

Find These Breeds:

ANDALUSIAN	APPALOOSA	CASPIAN	CLYDESDALE
CRIOLLO	FALABELLA	FRIESIAN	HACKNEY
LIPIZANNER	MORGAN	PALOMINO	PINTO
SHETLAND	SHIRE	THOROUGHBRED	WELSH

Chapter 2, page 58

Overo

Tobiano

Tovero

Chapter 3, page 78

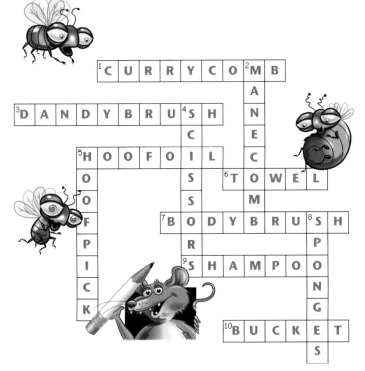

¹C	U	R	R	Y	C	O	²M	B		

¹CURRYCOMB
²MANECCMB
³DANDYBRUSH
⁴SCISSORS
⁵HOOFOIL
⁶TOWEL
⁷BODYBRUSH
⁸SPONGE
⁹SHAMPOO
¹⁰BUCKETS
HOOFPICK

Chapter 3, page 91-92

This is a type of horse that is neither light, nor heavy

P O N Y

This is the name used for finding out how old a horse is by looking at his teeth

A G I N G

Leather straps that help control the horse's movement

R E I N S

This kind of horse runs full blast around a track

R A C E H O R S E

Injury caused by the hind hoof toe striking the front heel

O V E R R E A C H

Faster than a walk, but slower than a run

T R O T

The hair on the horse's neck

M A N E

A horse of many, many years

O L D

(continued on next page)

Two letter abbreviation for the country where the American Quarter Horse and Appaloosa breeds originated

U   S

Horse equipment

T   A   C   K

Part of the horse that is shoed

H   O   O   F

A horse person

E   Q   U   E   S   T   R   I   A   N

The female parent of a horse

D   A   M

Final mystery clue:

This is a hyphenated word that describes a horse with an overbite.

P   A   R   R   O   T   _   M   O   U   T   H   E   D

Chapter 4, page 128

Use your knowledge about the life cycle of Strongyle larvae (worms) to complete the following sentences.

Fill in the missing words to complete the basic steps of a worm's life cycle:

Step 1

The ___**HORSE**___ eats then swallows the ___**STRONGYLE**___ ___**LARVAE**___ living in grass, ___**FEED**___, and water.

Step 2

The ___**LARVAE**___ lives in the horse's gut or ___**BLOODSTREAM**___ until it matures into an ___**ADULT**___ and lays its ___**EGGS**___.

Step 3

The ___**EGGS**___ leave the horse's body in a ___**MANURE**___ drop.

Step 4

The eggs ___**HATCH**___ in the manure resting on the ___**GROUND**___ and the ___**CYCLE**___ is ready to start all over again!

Chapter 5, page 143

True or False?
(Write T or F in each bale of hay)

 Your horse's weight isn't important when it comes to feeding.

 It's a good idea to make sure your horse likes his feed before buying a large amount.

 Feed in equal amounts at the same time each day.

 Keep feed bins off the ground but much higher than the horse's shoulders.

 Feed good hay like alfalfa because it is high in energy, protein, and calcium.

Appendix A: Answer Keys for Chapters 2-7

Chapter 5, page 157

Daily Drinkers

Use the key below to count how many quarts and gallons of water a horse needs to drink each day. *(4 quarts = 1 gallon)*

Quarts _____ Gallons __10__

Horsemen need much less water to survive than a horse does. Count how many quarts a horseman needs to drink each day.

Quarts: __2__ Gallons: _____

How many more quarts and gallons does a horse need to drink each day? *(Think subtraction!)*

Quarts: __38__ Gallons: __9.5__

Answer Key: Horse (40 quarts or 10 gallons); Horseman (2 quarts or .5 gallons); Quarts: (38); Gallons: (9.5 or nine and one-half)

Key

Gallon Quart

Chapter 5, page 164

Novice (easy)

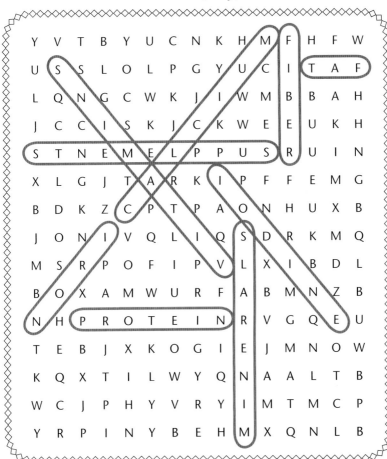

Find These words:

CALCIUM	FAT	FIBER
IODINE	IRON	MINERALS
PROTEIN	SUPPLEMENTS	VITAMINS

Chapter 5, page 165

Seasoned (advanced)

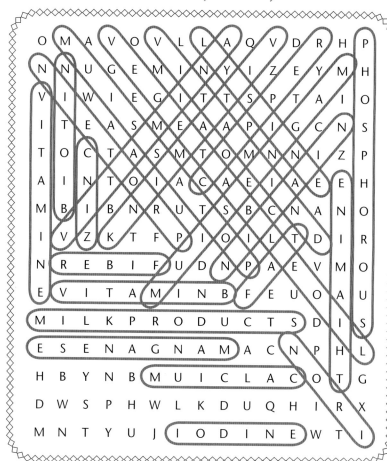

Find These words:

BIOTIN	CALCIUM	COPPER	ZINC
FAT	FIBER	IODINE	IRON
LYSINE	MAGNESIUM	MANGANESE	MILKPRODUCTS
NIACIN	PHOSPHOROUS	POTASSIUM	PROTEIN
THIAMINE	VEGETABLE OIL	VITAMIN A	VITAMIN B
VITAMIN D	VITAMIN E	VITAMIN K	

Chapter 6, page 175-176

Now that you know the basic horse gaits, step on out and put your new knowledge to work!

Read the following situations that a horse and rider could experience. Then fill in each blank with the gait that would be the best choice for each situation.

Fill the blank with the correct Gait:
Walk, Trot or Jog, Canter or Lope, Gallop, Back

1. You're rounding the last turn in a qualifying race.

Gait: __Gallop__

2. You're warming up your horse for a jackpot roping. After walking the arena a couple of times, you break into the next gait.

Gait: __Trot or Jog__

3. You are exercising your horse for a championship barrel race.

Gait: __Lope or Gallop__

4. You are leading a trail ride, traveling horseback on rocky, uneven ground.

Gait: __Walk__

5. You are warming up for a Western Pleasure class. Which gait will you use to check your horse's lead *(the foot used to step out and move the horse forward in the canter or lope)*?

Gait: __Cantor or Lope__

6. Your horse senses danger. No wonder! There's a snake's den close by and you need to calmly ease your horse away.

Gait: __Walk__

Chapter 7, page 231

Habits of Good Horsemanship	Reasons for Practicing Habits of Good Horsemanship
A. Wear a safety helmet	**D** Keep your horse clean and checked for anything that might cause him to be uncomfortable or harmed during a ride.
B. Wear shoes/boots with a heel	**F** In case of emergency, it's always a good idea for someone else to know your whereabouts!
C. Wear fitted and protective clothing	**E** A loose girth, twisted straps, or poorly fitting bridle and bit can cause big problems!
D. Groom and check horse before saddling	**C** Clothes should be fitted enough to not catch on anything, protective, and comfortable to ride in.
E. Check tack	**A** Protecting your head might save you from making a trip to the hospital.
F. Let someone know where you are riding, when you will return home, and who you are with.	**B** Heeled shoes/boots keep the foot safely in the stirrup. Leather soles are best because they slide in and out of the stirrup easily.

Appendix B

{ McREL Teaching Standards }

Chapter 1

ACTIVITY
Make Your Own Fossil *Hoof Print*
McREL National Standards:
- ★ **Language Arts** (Standard 7, Level III) Uses reading skills and strategies to understand and interpret a variety of informational texts: Uses new information to adjust and extend personal knowledge base
- ★ **Science** (Standard 7, Level II) Understands biological evolution and the diversity of life: Knows that fossils can be compared to one another and to living organisms to observe their similarities and differences
- ★ **Visual Arts** (Standard 2, Level II) Knows how to use structures and functions of art: Uses visual structures and functions of art to communicate ideas

ACTIVITY
How Many Hands Are You?
McREL National Standards:
- ★ **Language Arts**
  - (Standard 2, Level II) Uses the stylistic and rhetorical aspects of writing: Uses descriptive language that clarifies and enhances ideas
  - (Standard 5, Level II) Uses the general skills and strategies of the reading process: Establishes a purpose for reading (e.g., for information, for pleasure, to understand a specific viewpoint)
  - (Standard 7, Level II) Summarizes information found in texts (retells in own words)
- ★ **Math** (Standard 4, Level II) Understands and applies basic and advanced properties of the concepts of measurement: Selects and uses appropriate tools for given measurement situations
- ★ **Life Skills- Working with Others** (Standard 5, Level IV) Demonstrates leadership skills: Enlists others to work toward a shared goal

ACTIVITY
The Measure of a Miniature Horse
McREL National Standards:
- ★ **Language Arts** Standard 7, Level III) Uses reading skills and strategies to understand and interpret a variety of informational texts: Uses new information to adjust and extend personal knowledge base
- ★ **Life Skills- Self-Regulation** (Standard 1, Level IV) Sets and manages goals: Displays a sense of personal direction and purpose
- ★ **Visual Arts** (Standard 2, Level II) Knows how to use structures and functions of art: Uses visual structures and functions of art to communicate ideas

★ **Technology**
  • (Standard 2, Level I) Knows the characteristics and uses of computer software programs: Uses menu options and commands
  • (Standard 6, Level II) Understands the uses and different forms of technology: Knows that technology facilitates better communication by providing storage and retrieval of large amounts of data, an easy means of accessing data, a means of processing and displaying data, and faster communication skills among individuals

ACTIVITY
Ride the Pony Express!
McREL National Standards:
  ★ **Language Arts** (Standard 4, Level II) Gathers and uses information for research purposes: Uses multiple representations of information (maps, charts, photos, diagrams, tables, to find information for research topics
  ★ **History- Historical Understanding** (Standard 2, Level II) Understanding the historical perspective: Understands that specific decisions and events had an impact on history
  ★ **Physical Education**
  • (Standard 1, Level II) Uses mature form and appropriate sequence in combinations of fundamental loco-motor, object control and rhythmical skills that are components of selected modified games, sports, and dances
  • (Standard 5, Level II) Understands the social and personal responsibility associated with participation in physical activity: Works in a group to accomplish a set goal in both cooperative and competitive activities

ACTIVITY
Awesome Anatomy
McREL National Standards:
  ★ **Language Arts** (Standard 7, Level II) Uses prior knowledge and experience to understand and respond to new information
  ★ **Science** (Standard 5, Level II) Understands the structure and function of cells and organisms: Knows that living organisms have distinct structures and body systems that serve specific functions in growth, survival, and reproduction
  ★ **Life Skills- Working with Others** (Standard 1, Level IV) Engages in active listening; Demonstrates respect for others in group; Takes the initiative in interacting with others

ACTIVITY
Donkey Out-Horse In!
McREL National Standards:
  ★ **Language Arts**
  • (Standard 4, Level II) Organizes information and ideas from multiple sources in systematic ways

- (Standard 8, Level II) Responds to questions and comments
- ★ **Science** (Standard 5, Level II) Understands the structure and function of cells and organisms: Knows that living organisms have distinct structures and body systems that serve specific functions in growth, survival, and reproduction
- ★ **Life Skills- Working with Others** (Standard 1, Level IV) Engages in active listening; Demonstrates respect for others in group; Takes the initiative in interacting with others
- ★ **Technology**
  - (Standard 2, Level I) Knows the characteristics and uses of computer software programs: Uses menu options and commands
  - (Standard 6, Level II) Understands the uses and different forms of technology: Knows that technology facilitates better communication by providing storage and retrieval of large amounts of data, an easy means of accessing data, a means of processing and displaying data, and faster communication skills among individuals

Chapter 2

ACTIVITY
Horse Breeds Word Find
McREL National Standards:
- ★ **Language Arts**
  - (Standard 5, Level II) Uses the general skills and strategies of the reading process: Establishes a purpose for reading (e.g., for information, for pleasure, to understand a specific viewpoint); Uses personal criteria to select reading material
  - (Standard 7, Level II) Uses reading skills and strategies to understand and interpret a variety of informational texts: Summarizes and paraphrases information in texts

ACTIVITY
Face Markings: The Basics
McREL National Standards:
- ★ **Language Arts**
  - (Standard 4, Level II) Gathers and uses information for research purposes: Uses multiple representations of information
  - (Standard 5, Level II) Uses the general skills and strategies of the reading process: Uses word reference materials
- ★ **Visual Arts** (Standard 2, Level II) Knows how to use structures and functions of art: Knows the differences among visual characteristics and purposes of art (to convey ideas); Uses visual structures and functions of art to communicate ideas

ACTIVITY
The Mark of Champions
McREL National Standards:
- ★ **Language Arts** (Standard 8, Level II) Uses listening and speaking strategies for different purposes: Uses level-appropriate vocabulary in speech; Gives and responds to oral directions
- ★ **Life Skills- Working with Others** (Standard 1, Level IV) Engages in active listening; Demonstrates respect for others in group; Takes the initiative in interacting with others
- ★ **Technology**
  - (Standard 2, Level I) Knows the characteristics and uses of computer software programs: Uses menu options and commands
  - (Standard 6, Level II) Understands the uses and different forms of technology: Knows that technology facilitates better communication by providing storage and retrieval of large amounts of data, an easy means of accessing data, a means of processing and displaying data, and faster communication skills among individuals

ACTIVITY
Painted Patterns
McREL National Standards:
- ★ **Language Arts** (Standard 7, Level II) Uses Reading skills and strategies to understand and interpret a variety of informational texts: Summarizes and paraphrases information in texts; Uses prior knowledge and experience to understand and respond to new information
- ★ **Science** (Standard 4, Level II) Understands the principles of heredity and related concepts: Knows that many characteristics of an organism are inherited from its parents and other characteristics result with an individual's interactions with the environment
- ★ **History-Historical Understanding** (Standard 2, Level II) Understanding the historical perspective: Understands that specific decisions and events had an impact on history

Chapter 3

ACTIVITY
Shoebox Stable
McREL National Standards:
- ★ **Language Arts** (Standard 5, Level II) Uses the general skills and strategies of the reading process: Establishes a purpose for reading (e.g., for information, for pleasure, to understand a specific viewpoint); Reflects on what has been learned after reading and formulates ideas, opinions, and personal responses to texts

★ **Visual Arts** (Standard 2, Level II) Knows how to use structures and functions of art: Knows the differences among visual characteristics and purposes of art (to convey ideas); Uses visual structures and functions of art to communicate ideas

ACTIVITY
Could You Keep A Horse in Your Room?
McREL National Standards:
★ **Language Arts** (Standard 5, Level II) Uses the general skills and strategies of the reading process: Establishes a purpose for reading (for information, for pleasure, to understand a specific viewpoint)
★ **Math**
• (Standard 4, Level II) Understands and applies basic and advanced properties of the concepts of measurement: Understands the basic relationships between measures (length, perimeter, and area)
• (Standard 5, Level II) Understands and applies basic and advanced properties of the concepts of geometry; Understands that geometric shapes are useful for representing and describing real world situations
★ **Life Skills**- Thinking and Reasoning (Standard 4, Level II) Keeps a notebook that describes observations made; Distinguishes between actual observations and ideas or conclusions about what was observed

ACTIVITY
Tools of the Trade
McREL National Standards:
★ **Language Arts** (Standard 7, Level II) Uses reading skills and strategies to understand and interpret a variety of informational texts: Uses prior knowledge and experience to understand and respond to new information
★ **Behavioral Studies** (Standard 3, Level II) Understands that interactions among learning, inheritance, and physical development affect human behavior: Understands that many skills can be practiced until they become automatic, and that if the right skills are practiced, performance may improve

ACTIVITY
Hoof It!: Learn About and Label Hoof Parts
McREL National Standards:
★ **Language Arts** (Standard 7, Level III) Uses reading skills and strategies to understand and interpret a variety of informational texts: Uses new information to adjust and extend personal knowledge base
★ **Science** (Standard 5, Level II) Understands the structure and function of cells and organisms: Knows that living organisms have distinct structures and body systems that serve specific functions in growth, survival, and reproduction

ACTIVITY
Foil Horseshoes
McREL National Standards:

- ★ **Language Arts** (Standard 7, Level III) Uses reading skills and strategies to understand and interpret a variety of informational texts: Uses new information to adjust and extend personal knowledge base
- ★ **Science**
  - (Standard 5, Level II) Understands the structure and function of cells and organisms: Knows that living organisms have distinct structures and body systems that serve specific functions in growth, survival, and reproduction
  - (Standard 12, Level II) Understands the nature of scientific inquiry: Plans and conducts simple investigations to gather scientific data and extend the senses
- ★ **Visual Arts** (Standard 2, Level II) Knows how to use structures and functions of art: Uses visual structures and functions of art to communicate ideas

ACTIVITY
Horse Scramble
McREL National Standards:

- ★ **Language Arts** (Standard 5, Level II) Uses the general skills and strategies of the reading process: Previews text (e.g., skims material; uses pictures, textual clues, and text format); Establishes a purpose for reading (e.g., for information, for pleasure, to understand a specific viewpoint)
- ★ **Health** (Standard 7, Level I) Knows how to maintain and promote personal health: Knows personal hygiene habits required to maintain health (caring for teeth, gums, eyes, ears, nose, skin, hair, nails)

ACTIVITY
To Exercise or Not Exercise, That is the Question...or is it?
McREL National Standards:

- ★ **Language Arts**
  - (Standard 2, Level II) Uses the stylistic and rhetorical aspects of writing: Uses descriptive language that clarifies and enhances ideas
  - (Standard 5, Level II) Uses the general skills and strategies of the reading process: Establishes a purpose for reading (e.g., for information, for pleasure, to understand a specific viewpoint)
  - (Standard 7, Level II) Summarizes information found in texts (retells in own words)
- ★ **Health** (Standard 4, Level II) Knows how to maintain mental and emotional health: Knows the relationships between physical health and mental health
- ★ **Science** (Standard 12, Level II) Understands the nature of scientific inquiry: Plans and conducts simple investigations to gather scientific data and extend the senses

ACTIVITY
Horse'n Around with Concho Says!
McREL National Standards:
  * ★ **Language Arts**
    * (Standard 5, Level II) Uses the general skills and strategies of the reading process: Previews text (e.g., skims material; uses pictures, textual clues, and text format); Establishes a purpose for reading (e.g., for information, for pleasure, to understand a specific viewpoint)
    * (Standard 8, Level I) Uses listening and speaking strategies for different purposes: Gives and responds to oral directions; (Level II) Uses a variety of non-verbal communication skills
  * ★ **Physical Education** (Standard 1, Level II) Uses a variety of basic and advanced movement forms; Uses mature form and appropriate sequence in combinations of fundamental loco-motor, object control, and rhythmical skills that are components of selected modified games, sports, and dances
  * ★ **Life Skills**- Working with Others (Standard 1, Level IV) Engages in active listening; Demonstrates respect for others in group; Takes the initiative in interacting with others

Chapter 4

ACTIVITY
Handy Quick-Check Health Inventory
McREL National Standards:
  * ★ **Language Arts**
    * (Standard 7, Level III) Uses reading skills and strategies to understand and interpret a variety of informational texts: Uses new information to adjust and extend personal knowledge base
    * (Standard 8, Level II) Responds to questions and comments
  * ★ **Science** (Standard 12, Level II) Understands the nature of scientific inquiry: Plans and conducts simple investigations to gather scientific data and extend the senses
  * ★ **Life Skills- Thinking and Reasoning** (Standard 4, Level II) Distinguishes between actual observations and ideas or conclusions about what was observed

ACTIVITY
The Pinch Test for Dehydration
McREL National Standards:
  * ★ **Language Arts**
    * (Standard 7, Level III) Uses reading skills and strategies to understand and interpret a variety of informational texts: Uses new information to adjust and extend personal knowledge base
    * (Standard 8, Level II) Responds to questions and comments

★ **Science** (Standard 12, Level II) Understands the nature of scientific inquiry: Plans and conducts simple investigations to gather scientific data and extend the senses

ACTIVITY
IMPORTANT NUMBERS AND VITAL SIGNS
McREL National Standards:
  ★ **Language Arts**
    • (Standard 4, Level II) Gathers and uses information for research purposes: Use multiple representations of information (maps, charts, photos, diagrams, tables, to find information for research topics)
    • (Standard 5, Level II) Uses the general skills and strategies of the reading process: Establishes a purpose for reading (e.g., for information, for pleasure, to understand a specific viewpoint); Reflects on what has been learned after reading and formulates ideas, opinions, and personal responses to texts
  ★ **Science** (Standard 12, Level II) Understands the nature of scientific inquiry: Plans and conducts simple investigations to gather scientific data and extend the senses
  ★ **Life Skills- Thinking and Reasoning** (Standard 4, Level II) Keeps a notebook that describes observations made; Distinguishes between actual observations and ideas or conclusions about what was observed

ACTIVITY
Preparing an Equine First-Aid Kit
McREL National Standards:
  ★ **Language Arts**
    • (Standard 4, Level II) Gathers and uses information for research purposes: Use multiple representations of information (maps, charts, photos, diagrams, tables, to find information for research topics)
    • (Standard 5, Level II) Uses the general skills and strategies of the reading process: Establishes a purpose for reading (e.g., for information, for pleasure, to understand a specific viewpoint); Reflects on what has been learned after reading and formulates ideas, opinions, and personal responses to texts
  ★ **Science** (Standard 12, Level II) Understands the nature of scientific inquiry: Plans and conducts simple investigations to gather scientific data and extend the senses
  ★ **Life Skills- Thinking and Reasoning** (Standard 4, Level II) Keeps a notebook that describes observations made; Distinguishes between actual observations and ideas or conclusions about what was observed

ACTIVITY
In-a-Fix Horse Emergencies: Role Playing
McREL National Standards:
  ★ **Language Arts** (Standard 5, Level II) Uses the general skills and

strategies of the reading process: Establishes a purpose for reading (e.g., for information, for pleasure, to understand a specific viewpoint); Reflects on what has been learned after reading and formulates ideas, opinions, and personal responses to texts
★ **Behavioral Studies** (Standard 3, Level II) Understands that interactions among learning, inheritance, and physical development affect human behavior: Understands that many skills can be practiced until they become automatic, and that if the right skills are practiced, performance may improve

ACTIVITY
Horse Invaders: The Life Cycle of Larvae (worms)
McREL National Standards:
★ **Language Arts**
   • (Standard 5, Level II) Uses the general skills and strategies of the reading process: Establishes a purpose for reading (for information, for pleasure, to understand a specific viewpoint)
   • (Standard 7, Level III) Uses reading skills and strategies to understand and interpret a variety of informational texts: Uses new information to adjust and extend personal knowledge base
★ **Life Skills- Thinking and Reasoning** (Standard 4, Level II) Keeps a notebook that describes observations made; Distinguishes between actual observations and ideas or conclusions about what was observed
★ **Science** (Standard 5, Level II) Understands the structure and function of cells and organisms: Knows that living organisms have distinct structures and body systems that serve specific functions in growth, survival, and reproduction

ACTIVITY
Homemade Horsefly Trap
McREL National Standards:
★ **Language Arts**
   • (Standard 2, Level II) Uses the stylistic and rhetorical aspects of writing: Uses descriptive language that clarifies and enhances ideas
   • (Standard 7, Level II) Summarizes information found in texts (retells in own words). (Level III) Uses reading skills and strategies to understand and interpret a variety of informational texts: Uses new information to adjust and extend personal knowledge base
   • (Standard 8, Level II) Responds to questions and comments
★ **Science** (Standard 12, Level II) Understands the nature of scientific inquiry: Plans and conducts simple investigations to gather scientific data and extend the senses
★ **Life Skills- Thinking and Reasoning** (Standard 4, Level II) Distinguishes between actual observations and ideas or conclusions about what was observed

Chapter 5

ACTIVITY
Feeds and Feeding
McREL National Standards:
★ **Language Arts**
- (Standard 7, Level III) Uses reading skills and strategies to understand and interpret a variety of informational texts: Uses new information to adjust and extend personal knowledge base
- (Standard 7, Level II) Summarizes information found in texts (retells in own words)

ACTIVITY
Stall Feeding: How, What, When, Where, and Why for You Know Who
McREL National Standards:
★ **Language Arts** (Standard 5, Level II) Uses the general skills and strategies of the reading process: Establishes a purpose for reading (e.g., for information, for pleasure, to understand a specific viewpoint); Reflects on what has been learned after reading and formulates ideas, opinions, and personal responses to texts
★ **Science**
- (Standard 5, Level III) Knows that cell convert energy obtained from food to carry on the many functions needed to sustain life (cell growth and division, production of materials that the cell or organism needs)
- (Standard 6, Level II) Knows that the transfer of energy (through the consumption of food) is essential to all living organisms)

ACTIVITY
Horse Cuisine: Horse Healthy Treats
McREL National Standards:
★ **Language Arts**
- (Standard 5, Level II) Uses the general skills and strategies of the reading process: Establishes a purpose for reading (e.g., for information, for pleasure, to understand a specific viewpoint); Reflects on what has been learned after reading and formulates ideas, opinions, and personal responses to texts
- (Standard 7, Level II) Summarizes information found in texts (retells in own words)
★ **Science** (Standard 5, Level III) Knows that cell convert energy obtained from food to carry on the many functions needed to sustain life (cell growth and division, production of materials that the cell or organism needs)
★ **Life Skills: Life Work** (Standard 1, Level II) Makes effective use of basic tools: Measures and mixes dry and liquid materials in prescribed amounts, exercising reasonable safety

ACTIVITY
Water Watcher
McREL National Standards:
- ★ **Language Arts** (Standard 4, Level II) Gathers and uses information for research purposes: Uses multiple representations of information (maps, charts, photos, diagrams, tables, to find information for research topics)
- ★ **Science** (Standard 12, Level II) Understands the nature of scientific inquiry: Plans and conducts simple investigations to gather scientific data and extend the senses

ACTIVITY
Watering the Horse and Horseman
McREL National Standards:
- ★ **Language Arts** (Standard 4, Level II) Gathers and uses information for research purposes: Uses multiple representations of information (maps, charts, photos, diagrams, tables, to find information for research topics)
- ★ **Science**
  - • (Standard 5, Level II) Understands the structure and function of cells and organisms: Knows that living organisms have distinct structures and body systems that serve specific functions in growth, survival, and reproduction
  - • (Standard 12, Level II) Understands the nature of scientific inquiry: Plans and conducts simple investigations to gather scientific data and extend the senses
- ★ **Math** (Standard 3, Level III) Uses basic and advanced procedures while performing the processes of computation: Selects and uses appropriate computation methods for a given situation

ACTIVITY
An Amazing Body of Water: The Horseman
McREL National Standards:
- ★ **Language Arts** (Standard 5, Level II) Uses the general skills and strategies of the reading process: Establishes a purpose for reading (e.g., for information, for pleasure, to understand a specific viewpoint); Reflects on what has been learned after reading and formulates ideas, opinions, and personal responses to texts
- ★ **Math** (Standard 3, Level III) Uses basic and advanced procedures while performing the processes of computation: Selects and uses appropriate computation methods for a given situation
- ★ **Science** (Standard 12, Level II) Understands the nature of scientific inquiry: Plans and conducts simple investigations to gather scientific data and extend the senses

ACTIVITY
What's Fueling That Feed?
McREL National Standards:
- ★ **Language Arts**
  - (Standard 5, Level II) Uses the general skills and strategies of the reading process: Establishes a purpose for reading (e.g., for information, for pleasure, to understand a specific viewpoint); Uses personal criteria to select reading material
  - (Standard 7, Level II) Uses reading skills and strategies to understand and interpret a variety of informational texts: Summarizes and paraphrases information in text
- ★ **Health** (Standard 6, Level II) Understands essential concepts about nutrition and diet: Knows healthy eating practices; knows factors that influence food choices

ACTIVITY
One Lick, Two Licks, Three Licks, Four
McREL National Standards:
- ★ **Language Arts** (Standard 7, Level II) Uses reading skills and strategies to understand and interpret a variety of informational texts: Summarizes and paraphrases information in text
- ★ **Science** (Standard 12, Level II) Understands the nature of scientific inquiry: Plans and conducts simple investigations to gather scientific data and extend the senses
- ★ **Health** (Standard 6, Level II) Understands essential concepts about nutrition and diet: Knows healthy eating practices; knows factors that influence food choices

Chapter 6

ACTIVITY
Rhythm of the Gaits
McREL National Standards:
- ★ **Language Arts** (Standard 5, Level II) Uses the general skills and strategies of the reading process: Establishes a purpose for reading (e.g., for information, for pleasure, to understand a specific viewpoint); Reflects on what has been learned after reading and formulates ideas, opinions, and personal responses to texts
- ★ **Behavioral Studies** (Standard 3, Level II) Understands that interactions among learning, inheritance, and physical development affect human behavior: Understands that many skills can be practiced until they become automatic, and that if the right skills are practiced, performance may improve

ACTIVITY
Fill-In the Gait
McREL National Standards:
  - ★ Language Arts
    - • (Standard 7, Level III) Uses reading skills and strategies to understand and interpret a variety of informational texts: Uses new information to adjust and extend personal knowledge base
    - • (Standard 8, Level II) Responds to questions and comments
  - ★ **Life Skills- Thinking and Reasoning** (Standard 4, Level II) Distinguishes between actual observations and ideas or conclusions about what was observed

ACTIVITY
The Gallop Group Game
McREL National Standards:
  - ★ **Language Arts** (Standard 5, Level II) Uses the general skills and strategies of the reading process: Establishes a purpose for reading (e.g., for information, for pleasure, to understand a specific viewpoint)
  - ★ **Life Skills- Thinking and Reasoning** (Standard 4, Level II) Distinguishes between actual observations and ideas or conclusions about what was observed
  - ★ **Behavioral Studies** (Standard 3, Level II) Understands that interactions among learning, inheritance, and physical development affect human behavior: Understands that many skills can be practiced until they become automatic, and that if the right skills are practiced, performance may improve

ACTIVITY
Saddle Up, Partner!
McREL National Standards:
  - ★ **Language Arts** (Standard 4, Level II) Gathers and uses information for research purposes: Use multiple representations of information (maps, charts, photos, diagrams, tables, to find information for research topics)
  - ★ **Life Skills- Thinking and Reasoning** (Standard 3, Level II) Effectively uses mental processes that are based on identifying similarities and differences (compares, contrasts, classifies): Orders information based on importance of a given criteria; Compares different sources of information for the same topic in terms of basic similarities and differences
  - ★ **Visual Arts** (Standard 2, Level II) Knows how to use structures and functions of art: Knows the differences among visual characteristics and purposes of art (to convey ideas); Uses visual structures and functions of art to communicate ideas

ACTIVITY
The Imaginary Arena: Performance Fun
McREL National Standards:
  - ★ **Language Arts** (Standard 7, Level II) Uses reading skills and

strategies to understand and interpret a variety of informational texts: Uses prior knowledge and experience to understand and respond to new information
★ **Behavioral Studies** (Standard 3, Level II) Understands that interactions among learning, inheritance, and physical development affect human behavior: Understands that many skills can be practiced until they become automatic, and that if the right skills are practiced, performance may improve

ACTIVITY
A Bit about Head Gear
McREL National Standards:
★ **Language Arts** (Standard 5, Level II) Uses the general skills and strategies of the reading process: Establishes a purpose for reading (e.g., for information, for pleasure, to understand a specific viewpoint)
★ **Math** (Standard 4, Level II) Understands and applies basic and advanced properties of the concepts of measurement: Selects and uses appropriate tools for given measurement situations
★ Life Skills
★ **Working with Others** (Standard 5, Level IV) Demonstrates leadership skills: Enlists others to work toward a shared goal
★ **Thinking and Reasoning** (Standard 3, Level II) Effectively uses mental processes that are based on identifying similarities and differences (compares, contrasts, classifies):

ACTIVITY
Puzzling Pictures
McREL National Standards:
★ **Language Arts** (Standard 5, Level II) Uses the general skills and strategies of the reading process: Establishes a purpose for reading (e.g., for information, for pleasure, to understand a specific viewpoint); Reflects on what has been learned after reading and formulates ideas, opinions, and personal responses to texts
★ **Visual Arts** (Standard 2, Level II) Knows how to use structures and functions of art: Knows the differences among visual characteristics and purposes of art (to convey ideas); Uses visual structures and functions of art to communicate ideas

ACTIVITY
Rate-a-Horse
McREL National Standards:
★ **Language Arts**
  • (Standard 2, Level II) Uses the stylistic and rhetorical aspects of writing: Uses descriptive language that clarifies and enhances ideas
  • (Standard 8, Level II) Responds to questions and comments
★ **Science** (Standard 12, Level II) Understands the nature of scientific inquiry: Plans and conducts simple investigations to gather scientific data and extend the senses

★ **Life Skills- Thinking and Reasoning** (Standard 4, Level II) Distinguishes between actual observations and ideas or conclusions about what was observed

ACTIVITY
The Next Best Thing: The Mop Horse
McREL National Standards:
- ★ **Language Arts** (Standard 8, Level II) Uses listening and speaking strategies for different purposes: Uses level-appropriate vocabulary in speech; Gives and responds to oral directions
- ★ **Life Skills- Working with Others** (Standard 1, Level IV) Engages in active listening; Demonstrates respect for others in group; Takes the initiative in interacting with others
- ★ **Behavioral Studies** (Standard 3, Level II) Understands that interactions among learning, inheritance, and physical development affect human behavior: Understands that many skills can be practiced until they become automatic, and that if the right skills are practiced, performance may improve

ACTIVITY
Congratulations, First Place Junior Master Horseman!
McREL National Standards:
- ★ **Language Arts**
  - (Standard 7, Level III) Uses reading skills and strategies to understand and interpret a variety of informational texts: Uses new information to adjust and extend personal knowledge base
  - (Standard 8, Level II) Uses listening and speaking strategies for different purposes: Gives and responds to oral directions
- ★ **Life Skills- Working with Others** (Standard 1, Level IV) Engages in active listening

Chapter 7

ACTIVITY
Basic Horsemanship: Mount Up!
McREL National Standards:
- ★ **Language Arts** (Standard 7, Level II) Uses reading skills and strategies to understand and interpret a variety of informational texts: Uses prior knowledge and experience to understand and respond to new information
- ★ **Behavioral Studies** (Standard 3, Level II) Understands that interactions among learning, inheritance, and physical development affect human behavior: Understands that many skills can be practiced until they become automatic, and that if the right skills are practiced, performance may improve

ACTIVITY
The Emergency or Unexpected Dismount
McREL National Standards:
- ★ **Language Arts** (Standard 5, Level II) Uses the general skills and strategies of the reading process: Establishes a purpose for reading (e.g., for information, for pleasure, to understand a specific viewpoint); Reflects on what has been learned after reading and formulates ideas, opinions, and personal responses to texts
- ★ **Physical Education** (Standard 1, Level II) Uses mature form and appropriate sequence in combinations of fundamental loco-motor, object control and rhythmical skills that are components of selected modified games, sports, and dances
- ★ **Behavioral Studies** (Standard 3, Level II) Understands that interactions among learning, inheritance, and physical development affect human behavior: Understands that many skills can be practiced until they become automatic, and that if the right skills are practiced, performance may improve

ACTIVITY
A Quick Lesson in Horse Talk
McREL National Standards:
- ★ **Language Arts**
  - (Standard 7, Level III) Uses reading skills and strategies to understand and interpret a variety of informational texts: Uses new information to adjust and extend personal knowledge base
  - (Standard 8, Level II) Responds to questions and comments
- ★ **Life Skills- Thinking and Reasoning** (Standard 4, Level II) Distinguishes between actual observations and ideas or conclusions about what was observed
- ★ **Technology**
  - (Standard 2, Level I) Knows the characteristics and uses of computer software programs: Uses menu options and commands
  - (Standard 6, Level II) Understands the uses and different forms of technology: Knows that technology facilitates better communication by providing storage and retrieval of large amounts of data, an easy means of accessing data, a means of processing and displaying data, and faster communication skills among individuals

ACTIVITY
Habits of Good Horsemanship
McREL National Standards:
- ★ **Language Arts** (Standard 4, Level II) Gathers and uses information for research purposes: Uses multiple representations of information (maps, charts, photos, diagrams tables) to find information for research topics
- ★ **Thinking and Reasoning** (Standard 3, Level II) Effectively uses mental processes that are based on identifying similarities and differences (compares, contrasts, classifies): Orders information

based on importance of a given criteria; Compares different sources of information for the same topic in terms of basic similarities and differences
★ **Technology**
  • (Standard 2, Level I) Knows the characteristics and uses of computer software programs: Uses menu options and commands
  • (Standard 6, Level II) Understands the uses and different forms of technology: Knows that technology facilitates better communication by providing storage and retrieval of large amounts of data, an easy means of accessing data, a means of processing and displaying data, and faster communication skills among individuals

ACTIVITY
JMH Pledge
McREL National Standards:
★ **Language Arts** (Standard 8, Level II) Uses listening and speaking strategies for different purposes: Uses level-appropriate vocabulary in speech; Gives and responds to oral directions
★ **Life Skills- Working with Others** (Standard 1, Level IV) Engages in active listening; Demonstrates respect for others in group; Takes the initiative in interacting with others
★ **Behavioral Studies** (Standard 3, Level II) Understands that interactions among learning, inheritance, and physical development affect human behavior: Understands that many skills can be practiced until they become automatic, and that if the right skills are practiced, performance may improve

ACTIVITY
Ready, set ... Quick-Release Knot!
McREL National Standards:
★ **Language Arts** (Standard 4, Level II) Gathers and uses information for research purposes: Uses multiple representations of information (maps, charts, photos, diagrams tables) to find information for research topics
★ **Behavioral Studies** (Standard 3, Level II) Understands that interactions among learning, inheritance, and physical development affect human behavior: Understands that many skills can be practiced until they become automatic, and that if the right skills are practiced, performance may improve

ACTIVITY
How to Safely Pick Up a Horse's Foot
McREL National Standards:
★ **Language Arts** (Standard 7, Level III) Uses reading skills and strategies to understand and interpret a variety of informational texts: Uses new information to adjust and extend personal knowledge base
★ **Behavioral Studies** (Standard 3, Level II) Understands

that interactions among learning, inheritance, and physical development affect human behavior: Understands that many skills can be practiced until they become automatic, and that if the right skills are practiced, performance may improve
★ **Life Skills- Working with Others** (Standard 1, Level IV) Engages in active listening; Demonstrates respect for others in group; Takes the initiative in interacting with others

ACTIVITY
JMH Door Knob Hanger
McREL National Standards:
★ **Language Arts** (Standard 2, Level II) Uses the stylistic and rhetorical aspects of writing: Uses descriptive language that clarifies and enhances ideas
★ **Visual Arts** (Standard 2, Level II) Knows how to use structures and functions of art: Knows the differences among visual characteristics and purposes of art (to convey ideas); Uses visual structures and functions of art to communicate ideas

Chapter 8

ACTIVITY
JMH Traders Day
McREL National Standards:
★ **Language Arts** (Standard 4, Level II) Gathers and uses information for research purposes: Uses multiple representations of information (maps, charts, photos, diagrams tables, to find information for research topics)
★ **Thinking and Reasoning** (Standard 3, Level II) Effectively uses mental processes that are based on identifying similarities and differences (compares, contrasts, classifies): Orders information based on importance of a given criteria; Compares different sources of information for the same topic in terms of basic similarities and differences
★ **Life Skills- Working with Others** (Standard 5, Level IV) Demonstrates leadership skills: Enlists others to work toward a shared goal

ACTIVITY
Move 'Em Up, Head 'Em Out!
McREL National Standards:
★ **Language Arts** (Standard 8, Level II) Uses listening and speaking strategies for different purposes: Uses level-appropriate vocabulary in speech; Gives and responds to oral directions

★ **Life Skills- Working with Others** (Standard 1, Level IV)
Engages in active listening; Demonstrates respect for others in
group; Takes the initiative in interacting with others
★ **Behavioral Studies** (Standard 3, Level II) Understands
that interactions among learning, inheritance, and physical
development affect human behavior: Understands that many skills
can be practiced until they become automatic, and that if the
right skills are practiced, performance may improve

ACTIVITY
JMH Horse Drivers License
McREL National Standards:

★ **Language Arts** (Standard 8, Level II) Uses listening and speaking
strategies for different purposes: Uses level-appropriate vocabulary
in speech; Gives and responds to oral directions
★ **Life Skills- Working with Others** (Standard 1, Level IV)
Engages in active listening; Demonstrates respect for others in
group; Takes the initiative in interacting with others
★ **Behavioral Studies** (Standard 3, Level II) Understands
that interactions among learning, inheritance, and physical
development affect human behavior: Understands that many skills
can be practiced until they become automatic, and that if the
right skills are practiced, performance may improve

ACTIVITY
JMH Chuck Wagon Recipes
McREL National Standards:

★ **Language Arts** (Standard 5, Level II) Uses the general skills
and strategies of the reading process: Previews text (e.g., skims
material; uses pictures, textual clues, and text format); Establishes
a purpose for reading (e.g., fo r information, for pleasure, to
understand a specific viewpoint)
★ **History- Historical Understanding** (Standard 2, Level II)
Understands the historical perspective: Understands that specific
ideas had an impact on history
★ **Math** (Standard 4, Level II) Understands and applies basic and
advanced properties of the concepts of measurement: Selects and
uses appropriate tools for given measurement situations
★ **Life Skills: Life Work** (Standard 1, Level II) Makes effective use
of basic tools: Measures and mixes dry and liquid materials in
prescribed amounts, exercising reasonable safety

ACTIVITY
DVM Interview
McREL National Standards:

★ **Language Arts**
• (Standard 4, Level II) Gathers and uses information for research
purposes: Use multiple representations of information (maps,
charts, photos, diagrams, tables, to find information for research
topics)

- (Standard 5, Level II) Uses the general skills and strategies of the reading process: Establishes a purpose for reading (e.g., for information, for pleasure, to understand a specific viewpoint); Reflects on what has been learned after reading and formulates ideas, opinions, and personal responses to texts
★ **Science** (Standard 12, Level II) Understands the nature of scientific inquiry: Plans and conducts simple investigations to gather scientific data and extend the senses
★ **Technology**
    - (Standard 2, Level I) Knows the characteristics and uses of computer software programs: Uses menu options and commands
    - (Standard 6, Level II) Understands the uses and different forms of technology: Knows that technology facilitates better communication by providing storage and retrieval of large amounts of data, an easy means of accessing data, a means of processing and displaying data, and faster communication skills among individuals

ACTIVITY
Western Artist: Your Career Begins Here!
McREL National Standards:
- ★ **Language Arts** (Standard 7, Level III) Uses reading skills and strategies to understand and interpret a variety of informational texts: Uses new information to adjust and extend personal knowledge base
- ★ **Math** (Standard 4, Level II) Understands and applies basic and advanced properties of the concepts of measurement: Selects and uses appropriate tools for given measurement situations
- ★ **Life Skills: Life Work** (Standard 1, Level II) Makes effective use of basic tools: Measures and mixes dry and liquid materials in prescribed amounts, exercising reasonable safety
- ★ **Self-Regulation** (Standard 1, Level IV) Sets and manages goals: Displays a sense of personal direction and purpose
- ★ **Visual Arts** (Standard 2, Level II) Knows how to use structures and functions of art: Uses visual structures and functions of art to communicate ideas

ACTIVITY
Horse Industry Career Word Scramble
McREL National Standards:
- ★ **Language Arts** (Standard 7, Level III) Uses reading skills and strategies to understand and interpret a variety of informational texts: Uses new information to adjust and extend personal knowledge base
- ★ **Thinking and Reasoning** (Standard 3, Level II) Effectively uses mental processes that are based on identifying similarities and differences (compares, contrasts, classifies): Orders information based on importance of a given criteria; Compares different

sources of information for the same topic in terms of basic similarities and differences

★ **Technology**
  • (Standard 2, Level I) Knows the characteristics and uses of computer software programs: Uses menu options and commands
  • (Standard 6, Level II) Understands the uses and different forms of technology: Knows that technology facilitates better communication by providing storage and retrieval of large amounts of data, an easy means of accessing data, a means of processing and displaying data, and faster communication skills among individuals

Acknowledgements

American Youth Horse Council (AYHC) for the use of the Horse Industry Handbook

American Quarter Horse Association (AQHA) for underwriting and coordinating the project

Photographs provided by:

American Quarter Horse Association (AQHA)
American Quarter Horse Journal
American Paint Horse Association (APHA)
Arabian Horse Association (AHA)
Appaloosa Horse Club (ApHC)
Palomino Horse Breeders of America (PHBA)
American Miniature Horse Association (AMHA)
United States Pony Clubs (USPC)
Tennessee Walking Horse Association (TWHA)

Pilot Sites

STATE	NAME	SETTING
Arizona	Jaiene Marlow	Classroom
British Colombia	Leann Pitman	4-H Horse Club
Colorado	Kerith Gray	RMQHYA
Idaho	Kellie English	QHYA/Boys& Girls Club
Idaho	Anne Hughes	Black Canyon Ranch
Louisiana	Brenda Shope	4-H Horse Club
Mississippi	Gina Wills	4-H
Nevada	Patty Loveland	NQHYA
New Hampshire	Marge Tanner	4-H
New Jersy	Bronwyn Pait	NJQHYA
New York	Peggy Schuster	4-H
North Carolina	Polly Riddell	home
Oklahoma	Grant James	Trail Blazers Horse Club
Oklahoma	Donna Patterson	4-H Youth
Oregon	Mary Dunn	Extension
Tennessee	Linda A. Simmons	Back Nine Farms
Texas	Kim Riddle	Extension

Chapter 1—History
Amanda Rogers, NC, Victory Junction Gang Camp

Chapter 2 – Breeds & Classes
Amanda Rogers, NC, Victory Junction Gang Camp

Pat Comerford, PA
Extension Horse Specialist, Penn State University

Leslie Lange, CO
AQHA Horsewoman of the Year and Youth Activities
Committee member

Chapter 3 – Maintenance
John Magness, OK
Agriculture Teacher, Anadarko High School

Dr. Jason L. Turner, NM
Extension Horse Specialist, Department of Animal & Range Sciences
New Mexico State University

Chapter 4 – Health
Pete G. Gibbs, TX
Professor & Extension Horse Specialist
Department of Animal Science, Texas A&M University

Chapter 5 – Nutrition
David Freeman, OK
Professor of Animal Science, Oklahoma State University

Chapter 6 – Performance
Dr. Steven Cooper, OK
Associate Professor, Oklahoma State University

Norm Luba, KY
Executive Director , North American Equine Ranching Council

Kent Sturman, CO
Executive Director
National High School Rodeo Association

Leslie Lange, CO
AQHA Horsewoman of the Year and
Youth Activities Committee member

Chapter 7 – Safety
Rebekah Bachman, TX
West Texas A&M University

Chapter 8 – Life Skills and Career
Brenda Lacey, CA
4-H Program Representative
University of California, Cooperative Extension

Kristin Stutz, TX
Senior Director of Medical Education
Texas Tech University Health Sciences Center

Steering Committee

Justin Bisel, Past AQHYA Pres, Mount Vernon, OH

Lisa Hannewyk, Past AQHYA Pres, Niles, MI

Dr. Amber Crossland, Dripping Spgs, TX

Sheila Forbes, Stillwater, OK

Brenda Lacey, Independence, CA

Norm Luba, Louisville, KY

Jill Montgomery, AYHC—Pueblo West, CO

Marilyn Randall, Bridger, MT

Amanda Rogers, Greensboro, NC

Cookie Stude, Wright City, MO

Laurel Capurro-Wachtel, Deeth, NV

Dr. Doug Welsh, College Station, TX

Erin Randall, Palating, IL

Author

Teri Vestal, Teri Vestal Writing Productions, Odessa, TX

Graphic Design and Layout

Jackson Price, JP Creative, Chicago, IL

Project Management

Matthew Hutchings, Connexion Enterprises, Denver, CO

Debbie Gehring

Internet Production and Management

Will and Liz Wright, Willthing and Backyard Web Design, Amarillo, TX

AQHA Support

2005—2006 Executive Committees

    Frank "Scoop" Vessels, Past President

    Frank Howell, President

    Walter Fletcher, First Vice President

    Frank Merrill, Second Vice President

    Ken Mumy, Member

    Jim Helzer, Member

AQHA Staff

Bill Brewer, Executive Vice President

Don Treadway, Executive Director of Marketing

Ward Stutz, Director of Membership Services and Public Policy

Christy Bramwell, Sr. Manager of Youth Activities
and JMH Project Coordinator

Luann Ulrich, Assistant Manager of Communications and JMH Editor

DeAnna Carroll, Sr. Manager of E. Commerce Service